No Further West

NO FURTHER WEST

California Visited

Dan Jacobson

✦

THE MACMILLAN COMPANY
NEW YORK 1960

MADE AND PRINTED IN GREAT BRITAIN
IN 11 POINT BASKERVILLE
BY COX AND WYMAN LTD.
LONDON, FAKENHAM AND READING

Contents

→>-<-

Author's Note

THERE ARE REALLY, when you get down to it, only two kinds of anti-American: the foolish and the sinister. This book is not intended to give comfort to either. If I had not been heartened and exhilarated by what I saw in California, I would not have written about it—the effort would have been too great and the result would have been too dispiriting. I am aware that the first part of the book—in which I record so many things that distressed me—may appear to have a direct and concrete quality absent from some of the later and perhaps more encouraging chapters. But I can only say that ideas discussed in the latter half of the book did not come to me as abstractions—they were as much, for me, to be felt and encountered in personal terms as anything else in California, entering fully into the texture and immediacy of the life that was lived around me. If this had not been so, I could not have dealt with these ideas at all, for I can certainly make no claim to specialist knowledge of any aspect of American life or history. My account is throughout that of an interested visitor, and no more.

Though the ambition to write some kind of report of my experiences was born very early during my visit to California, I did not keep notes or a diary of any kind. Thus, with the exception of passages which originally appeared in an article in *The Reporter*, and the notes on the 'Beat Generation' which are taken from an article contributed to *Commentary*, this book is written entirely from recollection. For this reason I must ask the indulgence of the reader for any errors of fact or nomenclature of which I may have been guilty.

Acknowledgments are due to the editors of the two magazines mentioned above, and also to the editors of *Encounter* and *The Texas Quarterly*, in which some of the matter of the present book first appeared. I must also thank Professors Wallace Stegner and Richard Scowcroft of the English Department of Stanford University, for the award of the Fellowship which made possible my visit to California; and those American friends and neighbours who made the visit what it was.

D. J.

Part One

FIRST IMPRESSIONS

→>→<←

'WELCOME TO AMERICA!'

THE CURIOUS thing about air-travel is that it should be liberating, even inspiring; it should give one a sense of human power
and achievement; and it does nothing of the kind. This has
been remarked on often enough before; and the reason given
is simply that air-travel is, in some special and discreditable
way, 'modern'. The passengers in an aeroplane, we are told,
are sheep-like, faceless, harassed; the officials are indifferent
except when they are bullying; the whole process of travel on
the part of the passenger is never anything but one of sub-
mission, tedium, and a fear to which nobody admits. And then,
in a 'modern' way again, airports are supposed to be the same
all the world over—there is no distinguishing between them,
and for the traveller there is thus no real sense of movement: at
the end of a journey he finds himself in surroundings exactly
like those that were left behind at the beginning of the journey.
And for human warmth and friendliness among all this there
are the administrations of the air hostesses, with their mechanical smiles, their loud pert voices, their aloof strutting about
in their silly business-like uniforms. While on the flight itself,
instead of the variety and drama of the simplest train or boat
journey, there is only noise and vibration and nothing to see;
one is stuffed into one's padded seat and left to endure one's
boredom and anxiety, and those qualms in the pit of the
stomach caused either by the jolting of the plane or the meals
served on plastic trays.

Now all of this is true; yet it is only a half-truth, the other
half of the truth being that the reason for air-travel seeming so
stunned and tedious an activity is that what it *does* offer in the
way of variety and drama is too great for the mind to comprehend. It is not only the speed with which distances are crossed
that is meant here. It is something other than this from which
the passenger recoils into boredom and fatigue. Clouds lift
themselves in ranges, or are spread beneath the plane like a
floor or a thin shift through which the passenger is able to see

the minute serrations and indentations of the earth; but to
none of this is there any fixity or solidity, and what is furthest
seems most near, and yet there is nothing that is near. There is
only width upon width, distance upon distance, thin colour
upon colour, and light upon light: too much for any of us to
look at for long. So we look away, look at the magazines in
our hands, at our neighbours' weary faces, at the pastel-
coloured fixtures and fittings around us, at the hostess going
backwards and forwards, at the pilots and the navigator and
the engineer, the men into whose hands we have put our lives.
They know they are responsible for us, and though they are
bored too, doing their daily work, they enjoy their power and
responsibility and carry it flippantly. Beneath our boredom we
are afraid, and stir a little in our chairs when the engine changes
its beat or the plane rocks suddenly on an invisible gust or
pocket of air and we lose for a moment the sound of the engines.

So we flew from London to San Francisco, leaving London
at evening, and arriving in New York in the morning, after a
long reluctant dawn that had grown pale slowly, until there was
at last light enough for us to see more than one colour at a time;
beneath us we had seen the land to one side and the sea to the
other and between them a fine white strip of sand or foam.
Before that, in the middle of the night, there had been a stop at
Gander: a place all black, pierced by the tiny little electric
lights of a café into which we hurried out of the darkness and
the cold wind. There had been an elderly Canadian policeman
in a wooden box at the entrance to the café, who had danced
a little jig, snapping his fingers, when it was time for us to go.
'You folks better hurry,' he sang, and danced, like a queer
official sprite, the best that the night and the wind and the
Atlantic Ocean had been able to conjure up for us. There were
girls too, behind the counter of the café, but they neither sang
nor danced; they merely served coffee with the dulled, puffed
look of girls who should have been asleep. And then we had
hurried back to the plane, under a floodlight on the tarmac.

That was behind us, and so too was our reception at New
York, in a kind of tawdry, endless arcade, with the booths of the
various airline companies interspersed among shoe-shine establishments, money-changing counters, little eating places,
souvenir stalls—all of them low-ceilinged, brightly-lit, narrow

and crowded. In every ash-tray there were abnormally large cigarette-ends; half-cigarettes, three-quarter cigarettes, used for a moment and then discarded, even by the mechanics who sat about among the passengers, drinking their cool drinks and eating their sandwiches, very much at their ease. Of these people there hadn't been a sign at London airport; and there the cigarettes had been smoked down to their last fragments.

The Manhattan skyline we saw only from the air, toy-like, neat, the long narrow island anchored to the shores on both sides by little bridges. Then that was gone, and we flew over the America that unrolled itself like a map beneath us. There was the North-West, fertile, industrialized, thickly-populated; there were the Great Lakes, with Chicago in tiny blocks along the side of one of the lakes; there was the Middle West, the fields in squares and oblongs on the flat earth. There was a winding, leisurely river, brown and snake-like, and the hostess said, 'That's the Mississippi.' Then in wrinkles on the horizon, and later in warts and fissures nearer to us were the Rockies. Still we flew towards them, and even at the height we were flying some of the mountains were of a size that, trapped and liberated in our reaches of light and air, we could nevertheless recognize with awe. We flew over mountains, we flew over deserts, over the Salt Lake. Just as it had seemed earlier the day would never dawn, now it seemed that the same day would never end. The sun hung in the sky, ahead of us; it slipped a little lower; from a single golden sphere it became a tuft, a thing of long red rays, though there was nothing in the sky to which its rays could cling but our own plane. And we dozed, read, went to the drumming little lavatory, talked about the prices of cars to our fellow-passengers, while beneath us the map still rolled itself out and around us there was more transparent and uninhabitable space than we knew what to do with.

Then we were flying over country less mountainous and more inhabited. The little lights of habitation shone in clusters below us; and at last we came to a bay, a tongue of water that we knew for water because it was dark between the lights broadcast on both sides of it. The lights were white and orange and red and blue, lights like dust; and the plane dipped and sank and we left the air and came down to where it was darker than we had known it to be; we raced closely over the water, we bumped and bumped again; and the flight was over, we were in San Francisco, though London was barely a day behind us.

When we came out of the San Francisco Airport Terminal building, immediately in front of us there was a plain of parked cars—more parked cars than I had ever seen before in a single place, stretching in an unbroken expanse towards some kind of a bridge in the distance. Over the bridge there were other cars that moved in a continual procession, winding to the left and the right of the terrain of parked cars; and from the night-sky broken only by the chasing headlights there came the sound of the cars—a continual rustle, a fall of sound, a whisper out of the throat of the night. The cars glittered in front of us; they moved all about us, and above us, until where we stood seemed to be the centre of a circle of country that, as it gleamed and whispered, wheeled entirely around us. This was our first close sight of the country we had been flying over all day, our first true glimpse of what we thought of simply as America.

Then we were taken to a car, and we too began to move, as so many others were doing, around the plain of parked cars. The road we were on suddenly fell away in an arc, and then went up again, and around us other roads were rising and falling. Which road we were on I no longer knew—a broad black width of tar, tilted and curving, simply rushed towards our headlights, and by their lights I saw with a shock that neither our road nor any of the other roads were lying on rises or falls of the earth, but all were moving up from the ground or stepping down towards it on great concrete stilts. And these roads on stilts were wide, wide, and ran as fast as the headlights of our car, that travelled now towards another road wider than any we had yet seen, and flat before us. Then we were no longer tilted, but on a level with the big road; and though neither ours nor any of the other cars slowed down, we were moving on this road, and cars came past with a curiously close and confidential rustle at their rear wheels. In comparison with them, it seemed, we weren't travelling so very fast after all.

The cars were shining, swollen in front and at the back, coloured differently above and below; and never had I seen, never could I have imagined, so many of them moving so fast all

at one time. It was the movement, I suppose, that paralysed
the mind : one could have imagined cars, just cars, stretched out
indefinitely; but once they were set moving, at sixty or seventy
miles an hour, three or four abreast, in both directions, it
became too much, the imagination simply retreated and despaired, the mind was numbed.

In two directions, I have said; but there were more than two
directions that these cars travelled along. As we had joined the
big road by hurling ourselves at an angle into it, so other cars
were doing along other roads that came into ours from the right;
and so too roads suddenly sheered off to the right, and began to
climb on to structures that swung each road around in mid-air,
so that it crossed overhead, though the cars on it had a moment
before been racing pell-mell in front of our own. Now they
passed across in mid-air, treading on their rubber tyres, their
headlights shining. And on the other side of the road, as in a
mirror where everything was reversed, cars that had been
coming with their lights towards us, now crossed from left to
right above our heads. And again—as cars came from inclined
roads on our right, when they swam up and away from us,
swooped over us, came at angles towards us on the other side
of the road—the feeling was that not the cars but the roads
themselves were moving, like giant escalators moving at
speeds, ferrying hundreds of cars at a time, fast, fast, fast.

The road we had first entered along all those loops and slides
was the Bayshore Highway; the road where the car was
eventually parked was El Camino Real. El Camino Real was
the brighter of the two, the more sensational in the way of lights
and giant neon signs flickering names into the sky, but the less
remarkable as a feat of highway engineering, with fewer lanes
for traffic, fewer overpasses, underpasses, skyways, bridges and
all the rest of the massive works that accompany any American
freeway. But the first night they were, as far as I knew, one
great frightening road; and it was then that I first felt the
ambition to write some kind of a book about California. And
the substance of the book, the single message of the book would
be to the world outside California (and curiously enough, to the
Californians too) : *You don't know what it is like!* I hadn't known;
and when we stopped the car at the drive-in to have a bite to eat

I couldn't believe that the people at the drive-in knew what it was like. And 'it' was nothing less than California, nothing less than America, all the few miles of it that we had closely seen.

The drive-in was a circular place shaped like a spool, with the body of the spool made out of glass, so that one could see the cooks and the waiters at their work inside it. Through the middle of the spool there ran a kind of spindle, a tower, a mast that came out at the top and was decorated with stripes of bright white neon. The spindle revolved incessantly, each stripe flickering dazzlingly past the eye as it came round and round again. On the great wide road just a few paces off, cars hurled themselves one way and another, each car looking bigger and apparently travelling faster than the last; and all around the spool of the drive-in were more cars, momentarily at rest, the faces of the occupants flickering in the light of the spindle above. The drivers of these cars seemed all to be children. There were boys, babies, children, sitting at the wheels of these gigantic cars, and drinking their coffee and eating their doughnuts and triple-decker sandwiches. The children talked, they called to each other from car to car, while the waiters went in and out of the doors of the spool and various indistinct figures within worked over shining stoves and metal-topped tables. And there was no one there who saw anything remarkable in the drive-in and all its lights, or the fiercely busy highway stretching a few yards away from us like something flung open, or the cars that were passing, or the neon signs blazing at all the establishments near by; not a single child seemed to see anything remarkable in the fact that he should be sitting at the wheel of a car that was as large and decorated and considerably more powerful and comfortable than the chariot of an emperor. They seemed to take it all for granted; and in that way they didn't know what it was like.

I too began to take more and more things for granted, as the days and then the weeks and months passed, though I can say that not once did I take El Camino Real for granted; and still less the Bayshore Highway. Later we were to see on El Camino the shabbiness that the thousand neon signs hid from us on that first night; we were to see that many of the places we had passed were no more than shabby wooden lean-to's, or cheap jerry-built places false-fronted with brick, or rubbishy 'Spanish' establishments with plaster and arches and red-tiled roofs. But these sights were to come later. On the first night El Camino Real was all a wonder, an amazement; every motel or drive-in we passed was a place of light, bloated and palatial under the signs that stared and glared and gave to each one its name.

I had never seen anything like the highways that had taken us from the airport; but when at last we left the highway and turned into Palo Alto, the town where we were to stay, I felt I knew where I was again. The streets of the little town were quiet, tree-lined, half-lit by the street lamps; there were oleander bushes, and bluegum trees and pepper trees; and when we got out of the car in a quiet street, we heard the sound of the cicadas calling, a sound like the voice of summer itself. There was no cold in the air. After three years in England one expected—even in midsummer—to feel at that hour a breath of cold air coming from the ground, from the trunks of the trees, from the walls of the house we approached. But there was none; the air was like that of my home town in South Africa, Kimberley: it even had within it the faint dry smell of dust, though no breeze blew. The scent rose up as if warmth alone were enough to diffuse it everywhere.

But it was 'Welcome to America!' that our landlady cried from the porch as we approached her house. The professor from the university who had met us at the airport and brought us from there in his car seemed a little embarrassed at this greeting. He introduced us to the lady, who nodded and cried, 'You folks must be exhausted! Well, well, and who is this young man? And say, what a cute baby! Aren't you just the cutest baby? You certainly are the cutest baby I've ever seen.' We shook hands, and as we did so, she repeated, 'Welcome to America!'

She was a tiny, frail, elderly woman, whom we were to get to know fairly well in the time we were with her. Her body was bent, her legs were splayed, her hair hung in wisps over her forehead; age had withered her, all right, but custom could not stale her variety. On the first evening she seemed to see herself as nothing less than a presidential envoy welcoming us to America on behalf of America. At other times, however, she was to be a loving and well-loved grandmother; or a lonely and maltreated

B

widow-woman adrift in an incomprehensible modern world that she could not deal with at all; or an intellectual who took courses in what she called 'the behavioural sciences'; or a cheery old soul, full of wise sayings like, 'It doesn't do to fret and fuss,' or 'There's no calling back the times that are past and no telling the times that are to come'. She could be any of these people, and many more, at a moment's notice; but under them all she was as well, persistently, an imposer of obligations, a maker of promises that she could never keep, and an addle-head.

On the very first evening, for example, it was discovered that the lavatory given to us for our private use did not work. What exclamations there were from her, what deep stares into the cistern, what sighs at the robbers who passed themselves off as plumbers these days, what helpless feminine jigglings of the stop-cock, what head-shakings, what shakings of a tiny fist as she rehearsed the things she was going to say to that plumber-man! And the whole performance, we found out later from a fellow-lodger, was a piece of play-acting. No one could remember when that lavatory had last worked, it was a clogged, blocked, hope-less, smelly piece of machinery, that neither plumber nor lay-man had been near for years. But we did not know this the first evening. Then our landlady seemed just a quaint and rather sweet old lady who was anxious to do her best for us, a woman of enthusiasms who brought us cups of coffee, who brought toys for the children to cuddle down with, who refused to talk business because we-all were so tired and there was always time for business but never enough time for just a little friendliness.

In the following days it became practically an obsession with me to get out of her house, with its evil oily smell, its tattered furniture, its wide linoleum-covered passages, its filthy kitchen, its refrigerator that stretched across one wall of a kind of scullery and shook and roared by day and night—and all its other inhabitants, most of whom seemed to be connected with the landlady in some familial and incurably lame-dog way. There were women without husbands but many children, children with no parents at all, an idiot woman who lived in one of the bedrooms by day but emerged at night to watch television, a man who was apparently unhappily married to two women, a boy who had to wear a plaster cast on his hand from when he had beaten it against a wall in a fit of rage; in a cabin in the

back yard there was a woman who returned home every mid-
night, with her daughter asleep on the back seat of the car. We
learned early that everything in California was not hygienic
and expansive. In another shack further down in the back yard
there was a graduate student of history and his pregnant wife,
who had fallen in the landlady's hands, as we had, and were as
obsessional as we were about getting out of them. We became
friends with this couple, and remained friends; we'd sit in their
shack in the evenings, and exchange notes on the prospect of
being able to escape.

All this lay ahead of us. On the first night we were simply
grateful—as we still are—that the people at the university had
gone to the trouble of finding a place for us to stay. We were
content to stretch ourselves out for the first time in thirty hours
and fall asleep.

2

THE SEVERED TENDON

WHY HADN'T anyone *told* me? That was the question I asked of myself in awe, in fear, in anger, in despair. What I saw was all new, brand-new, and of a size and a populousness and a busyness that I couldn't begin to comprehend. Why hadn't anyone told me about it? Why hadn't I been warned?

And I asked this question though what we saw of Palo Alto by daylight on our first morning there confirmed my first impression that the town was very similar to the small towns I had known in South Africa. There was the same sense of space, newness, and sandiness; there were the same wide tarred streets, empty in the sun; there were the same lawns of grass shrivelling at the edges; the leaves of familiar trees hung down spiritlessly in front of houses that were often of a style I had known in South Africa; there was a main street, with its shop windows and department stores stretching away from the pavements, and few people about.

But the difficulty was that this main street wasn't main at all, and the town wasn't a small one, if it existed at all; and of that I wasn't sure. What I saw in the days following our arrival seemed to be a single sprawl that stretched all the thirty miles between San Francisco and Palo Alto and for another thirty miles beyond; and what it was anywhere along the length was precisely what it was anywhere else along its length. And what *that* was—I had no word for it. It was a sprawl, a mess, a nightmare of repetition and disjunction and incoherence, all grown permanent and powerful.

There were shops, identical houses in tracts, drive-ins, motels, factories, shopping centres, supermarkets, giant billboards, filling-stations, used-car lots all along El Camino Real. There were identical houses in tracts, drive-ins, motels, shopping-centres, supermarkets, giant billboards all along the Bayshore Highway; there were whole towns of identical houses in tracts between the Bayshore Highway and El Camino Real; and further again, and further yet, there were

used-car lots and giant billboards and shopping centres and
supermarkets . . .

And all the buildings sprawled wide, drunkenly, sharing no
style, no size, having no relation to one another but that imposed
on them by the single thing they did share: a frontage of the
road, a view of the traffic, a gaze across to the other side of the road
where there were other motels, drive-ins, gas-stations and other
names—The Crown, Crazy Jack's, Ole Olsen's, Top-T Service,
and a supermarket spaciously spelling out its name with a single
letter in each of its stucco arches. They were all spread away
from one another, pushed apart physically. Every car of the
thousands that rushed at all times and along all the length
of the roads had to have a place for it when it swung off the road
and stopped. So, sprawling enough in themselves, the places
spread their grounds wider still, in hope that one car or a hundred would stop in this drive-in rather than the fifty others
over the last few miles, this supermarket rather than the last.
Perhaps the car would stop because in front of this supermarket
someone had taken the trouble to advertise—in black letters
six inches high against a white illuminated background—
Celery: 10 Cents a Stick. How could anyone go to so much trouble
to sell sticks of celery, one wondered; but one wondered about
nothing very long on that road, because next there was a car
mounted on a platform twenty feet high, and slowly the whole
platform turned round, bearing the car on its palm. Below it,
and stretching away from it was a used-car lot, and another, all
decorated with streamers and bunting and strings of plastic
whirligigs, as if royalty were soon to pass by, to inspect the acres
upon acres of used cars, glittering in their lots on the sand. Then
a service-station, or two, or three, a motel with all its Swiss-
style gabled little chalets in a row along the road, a second-hand
furniture mart, a liquor store, more used-car lots. It was impossible to tell which of all the cars in rows belonged to one lot and
which to another, for there were no fences between them; but
there were names on poles, names on billboards, names as high
as the little wooden offices that bore them, and each name was
different from the last—unless it was a name that had been seen
before, fifty times before, in front of other lots, on other hoardings, further back along the road.

The used-car lots covered their spaces, they stretched down

the road, and then beyond them there rose the grandeur of a
new shopping centre. This one looked something like the Palais
de Chaillot in Paris. It was white, it gleamed, it flung its arms
open as if to embrace not a terraced garden but a plain of
parked cars as wide as that first one we saw in front of the
airport. These shopping centres were things that we had never
seen before—places that under a single sprawling roof housed
enough shops to supply the wants of a town. That one was like
the Palais de Chaillot; the next was quaint, rural, timbered,
with flagged walks, low buildings with overhanging eaves, at
every corner a loudspeaker playing soft music. In this shopping
centre there was a shop that sold only electronically-operated
garage doors; but otherwise there was nothing in it that was not
repeated shabbily or elegantly by some single shop belonging to
the sprawl directly and not through the *imperium in imperio* of the
shopping centre. They both contributed to the sprawl, and
who could say which contribution was the greater—that of the
shopping centre, with all its elegant arcades and galleries, or of
this shabby drive-in shaped like a Mexican hat, with its brim
over the place where cars were parked?

But what did shabby mean here, and what did elegant mean?
Here was a shack of shingles and nails all smeared and disfigured
with the great letters that give it its name—but within there
was wall-to-wall carpeting, marble-topped desks, mobiles
hanging from the ceilings, and sheer glass partitions; there was
a neon sign blazing away so fiercely that it almost hid the little
barn behind it where food was served. And the cars in the used-
car lots, were they shabby or are they elegant? And that
hospital for dogs, where on the roof a neon dog wagged its long
neon tail?

But it was gone too, behind us, in a moment, for one always
travelled by car down the roads, one never walked.

Those highways were able along their length to provide you
with any material thing you might ever need. There were all the
shops of various kinds; there were banks, travel-agencies,
money-lenders, real-estate agents who would sell you a house,
and furniture stores that would sell you the furniture to fill it
with. There were bookstores and shops selling the latest selection of records, and little establishments that offered tropical

fish in bowls, and imported Danish cutlery. There were the
shops and the facilities for whole cities of prosperous people; but
the curious, the frightening thing was that all the shops and
facilities belonged only to the highways and to no city.

Nowhere along their length did the highways seem to contract, confine themselves, centre themselves for a community
around them. There were no parks along the highways, no
statues, no plaques commemorating notable events; there were
no vistas, no views, no streets that radiated from this point or
that; there was nowhere that one could turn and look back the
way one had come. The highways ran with all their businesses
and townships from San Francisco to Palo Alto and beyond,
simply ploughing across the country; and it was as if some kind
of vital tendon had been severed, so that they could grasp
nothing to themselves, could enclose nothing in themselves,
could make no order of themselves, but could only lie sprawling,
incoherent, centreless, viewless, shapeless, faceless—offering all
the products a community might need and yet making the
establishment of a community impossible.

For it was by the roads and from the roads that the towns like
ours seemed to live. Every morning half of the male inhabitants
of the towns seemed to get into their cars and go thundering
along the highways to San Francisco or elsewhere, and every
evening they thundered back again. The women drove along
the highways to do their shopping; the very air of the towns was
filled night and day with the whisper of the traffic on the highways. As our town seemed to be, so seemed all the others—flat,
indistinguishable appendages to the highways, equal parts of a
brand-new nameless sprawl across a country.

3

PEOPLE AND POWER

IF THE BUILDINGS were so jumbled together that it was impossible to say of one area that it was rich and of another that it was poor, of one area that it was elegant and another that it was shabby; if expensive shops looked like lean-to's, and supermarkets like palaces; if the physical existence of all that I saw was bewildering and dazing and so without centre that a block away from the house where we boarded I might have been ten miles up the El Camino or twenty miles down the El Camino; if I was lost among things alone—what could I make of the people who lived among all these things, who had made them all, and who seemed to me as indistinguishable from one another as their houses in tracts, their roads, their gas-stations, the very clothes on their backs?

But before going on I should say that I come from what are probably—in their very different ways—two of the most caste-conscious societies in the Western world: South Africa and England. In South Africa the caste is a matter of colour: and there is no mistaking its gradations, its hierarchy, its organization. The position of each man is given to him at his birth, and even if he were to try his hardest to lose it, he could not, it would follow him. Among the whites it follows even those who sink below the level of the dark-skinned folk and become 'poor whites'. But they are still poor *whites*: drunken, in tatters, reeking and staggering about the country roads or streets of the towns, the poor white remains a white man, a member of the highest caste the society affords. So every member of each group recognizes another man firstly as a member of his group, and then only—possibly—as a man. And even among the whites there are the English, the Afrikaners, the Jews, the Greeks, all separate from one another; and among the non-whites there are the Africans, the Indians, the Coloureds, the Chinese; and each of these groups is above one group and below another, sharply and finally.

In England the distinctions are infinitely subtler, more diffi-

cult to classify, and there are more of them; but the English
class-system is fine, intimate, and all-pervasive; and though
it keeps the classes apart, it also cements them together, in a
curious familial bond. Despite the social changes in England
which have been so much talked about, it remains impossible
to look at English society but under the aspect of class, and
through a sense of class.

Now, even to an outsider, both the supple, inbred and intimate class-structure of England; and the rigid, fanatical colour-
structure of South Africa, are recognizable structures, ways of
ordering people, and their towns, their dress, their manners,
their speech, their relationships with one another. And whether
or not one is happy or unhappy about either or neither of the
orders imposed by these structures does not really matter in
this context. These were the orders, these were the societies
in which I had more or less known my way about, and through
which I had had to make my way. But here in California
there was—it seemed to me—no order, no society, no hierarchy,
no gradations, no class distinctions, no classes, no structure at
all. Just people. And more people. And more people again.

It was late summer in California, and the sun shone all day
upon all the things and buildings that have already been
catalogued and will not be catalogued again, in case the reader
gets weary. (But let the reader remember that there is no
way of describing an incoherent jumble but by cataloguing it;
and let him remember too that every catalogue that could be
given is after all just one—and along the El Camino and the
Bayshore Highway there was not one but a hundred occasions
for a hundred further catalogues. And let the reader imagine
himself tumbling out of an aeroplane into the middle of them,
and by no means should he forget that the sun came down upon
them in a yellow dazzle all the hours of daylight. By night, of
course, the dazzle was multi-coloured, and though less powerful, it moved more—in arrows, circles, dotted lines, cascades
of simulated water, and the waving arms of little neon men.)

Because the weather was so warm, the people then—as I
began to say—wore few clothes. The women for the most
part wore cotton dresses or thin blouses and skirts, or trousers;
the men wore shirts and trousers and shoes and socks; and
that was just about all. Many of the shirts were extremely

colourful, but a surprising number were khaki; and khaki long trousers were fashionable too. And those who did wear suits all wore light-weight suits, whose colours were generally discreet, pastel-shaded: light blues and light browns predominating. Now it is difficult to ascribe class of any kind to people who all dress much like each other; when they all wear light clothes and light colours like holiday-makers, it seems quite impossible.

And they all spoke much like each other. It is true that their accents varied; but the variations, from what I could tell, were casual, regional, and equal to one another. So they dressed alike, and they spoke to each other on equal terms. And they all drove motor cars which were of a size and a gaudiness that can be described—as they seemed to have been created —in terms of sheer fantasy only. My own fantasy is that the designers of these cars asked of themselves, before all else: What would a *nouveau-riche*, detribalized and probably drunken Arab chieftain who had just made a fortune out of oil (and a little slave-running on the side—the side nearest his heart) most want *his* car to look like when he took out an equally detribalized Arab chieftain for a spin after attending the Riviera party that celebrated the wedding of a Hollywood film-star to a Costa Rican tanker-millionaire? The technical success of these designers is witnessed to, I suppose, by the number of Arab chieftains who do in fact drive just such cars; but it was disconcerting to find that so did everyone else in California. And—as they say in California—when I say everyone I mean everyone. I mean roadbuilders and university professors and high-school children and the postman too.

They dressed alike, they spoke alike, and they all drove the same kind of motor car. And they all had the same kind of face. Now a lot of nonsense has been talked about the faces of Americans; we have been told that Americans have baby-faces, they have innocent faces, that they have no faces. But what was bewildering about the American faces that I saw in the first days of my stay was that there was none that looked like another; and, as with their accents, in a different way it was in this sense that they were paradoxically all alike. There seemed to be no standard, no type from which deviations could be judged: any one face was as good, and as American, as any other. This—I admit—is a difficult matter to generalize about without talking nonsense; especially since one thing I have become much aware of since my return to England is the wild eccentricity of the faces of the English. To walk down the high street of the nearest village here in Devon is to be convinced that one has fallen into a land of gnomes, witches, morons, kind fairies, hobgoblins. Yet despite this oddity of facial appearance somehow it is still possible to imagine an ideal 'English' face, or several ideal 'English' faces from which all real English faces happen to diverge accidentally. It is impossible to do this with an American face, or at least with the American faces we saw in the streets about us in California. 'They *look* such a mixture,' a fellow-alien said to me about the Americans about us; and that just about describes the impression they made: another mixture, another jumble, another catalogue called for.

They dressed alike, they spoke alike, they all drove the same bizarre and opulent kind of motor car, and any one face was as good as any other. And their manners were alike. They were casual enough: people said 'Hi!' to each other in greeting, with a sideways and backwards jerk of the head, as if shaking something free of themselves; yet despite this casualness and the surface helpfulness and friendliness that went with it, there was—it seemed to me—at the same time a watchful, withdrawn quality, that I hadn't expected. The American manner was direct enough, but it wasn't without its own kind of complexity. And beneath the watchfulness again there seemed to be a fundamental indifference, a blankness of response that could be disconcerting in the extreme. Sure they'd be of help if they could, sure they'd smile at me in a friendly fashion, sure they'd wonder at my accent and my clothing and try to guess whether or not I was a responsible citizen or a delinquent of some kind or another; and sure they'd forget all about me the moment they turned their backs on me. For there were too many people moving about for them to be concerned with any one person for too long, and I was not the only stranger in California. Indeed, California seemed to be populated with strangers. In the nine months we lived there I doubt if I met more than a dozen people who were Californian-born—there was a mobile, nomadic, newly-arrived air about almost everyone. So the newly-arrived greeted the yet-more-newly-arrived; and afterwards the wonder became not that there was indifference beneath the watchfulness, but that the watchfulness and the friendliness should have been as alert and as unfailing as it was, whatever there was beneath it.

And beyond all these difficulties of discrimination there was the greatest and most curious and newest difficulty of all: the difficulty of discriminating, of establishing the relationship, between the people and the things around them—the tens of thousands of haphazard, new, shoddy things among which the people lived, through which they made their way, and about which they seemed to care so much, to judge from the way they were building and making, more and more, every day, everywhere. Everyone was busy; but from all the busy-ness, from all the meetings and the greetings and farewells, from every activity I saw there seemed at first to come no order, only a further and wider and shallower and louder and uglier disorder. Among it I could not but feel lost, homeless; but what was new and frightening was the sense I felt of strangeness among the people who were already there—between the people and each other, between the people and the things they were making.

Yet there was another possibility that was still more frightening. Did these words that I used to describe my state and felt I could have used to describe the state of everyone around me— did these words have any meaning here? What did it mean to be homeless, when 'home' was one more wooden tract house behind a single wooden fence stretching the length of the tract, as if the whole estate were some kind of temporary camp? What did it mean to be 'lost' when you did not know what could be found among the jumbled catalogues of things spilled out along the highways? What were the meanings of the words here that in so new a country as South Africa and in so old a country as England I had learned to look for and value? These words that I use: community, structure, class, society, state, town—what meaning did any of them have in the Bay Area of San Francisco, in this Californian peninsula, in the fastest-growing area of the fastest-growing state of the United States? What meaning could they have? Or were they words that should be abandoned, as having served for other groups in other times, but being of no relevance to this conglomeration of peoples among a great conglomeration of ever-accumulating things, who needed new words, new forms, new modes to describe and order them, who would attain their order and their forms only when they had the new words? What were the words of value and the words for value here?

In everything I have written so far I have had the uneasy feeling that there is no one who will believe me when I tell him that he doesn't know what California is like. News from America? From California, of all states in America? If there is one country that any reader outside it believes he knows all about, it is the United States. He need never have crossed the Atlantic westwards or the Pacific eastwards, but nevertheless there is nothing in America that he thinks he does not know familiarly, and, often enough, despairingly. To the non-American 'America' is so often imagined as being merely what his own country is in every aspect but that for which his country is dear to him, every aspect but that of his country's own past. And the distaste the non-American so often feels for himself or his country in the present he believes he must feel for the United States as a whole. 'Give me your tired, your poor . . . the homeless, tempest-tossed,' they put at the bottom of the Statue of Liberty to welcome the immigrants in; but everyone is tired and tempest-tossed now, and feels himself to be under the dominance of that greenish uplifted arm even if he stays put where he is.

For if we all regard ourselves as Americans of a kind, we do not do so with any hope or favour—America is no promised land, no golden west, but the wasteland where we live. 'America'—we like to believe—is what is déjà vu, uprooted, nomadic, indiscriminate, faceless, shapeless; it is the uniformity that is spreading faster and faster over the whole habitable globe; it is the product and the market of the mass media of entertainment, with their debasement and deadening of every form of human expression; it is the disappearance of order and particularity and continuity in the life of the human individual and the individual society; it is the cramming of more and more people into an ever-closer contiguity that serves only to make each one of them more anonymous, discrete, incoherent, isolated, capable only of the most frictive and trivial relationships with his fellows; it is the way of life that makes it inevitable that among greater riches than he has ever enjoyed before man should be more miserable than ever before, uglier, less expressive, colder,

without spontaneity and without hope. All this is 'America', we
are given to insisting; and it is precisely the 'Americanization'
of the world that we see all too much of about us, wherever we
live.

So what then could be new about my news?

Only two things I believe. The first is that in California at
any rate, the physical pre-conditions for all this—all of it, and
more if you like, every black fear that we have ever had about
the way we are heading, everything we have been warned
against, every doom that every prophet of our culture has been
crying down upon us—these pre-conditions have already happened. They aren't things impending, threats, dangers for the
future. They are already here, one can visit them and walk
among them in California; one can watch their lights, hear
their noises, see their buildings, dodge their cars, buy their
goods, read their papers. And one can live among them.

That is the second item of news. It is a modest one; but one
worth recording. And it involves further warnings and guesses
and speculations, and also a little hope.

So stand with me on the Bayshore Highway, and let us look at
what we can see; and let us remember what we see whenever
we think of California. We will choose a place where there is a
road coming into the Bayshore Highway—something which is in
itself a little uncommon, for the Bayshore Highway is a freeway,
with restricted access. But here they have not built it as it will
be when it is finished; and here there is still an ordinary intersection, with a traffic light, as one might find anywhere else in
the world. Behind us, hundreds of yards down, there is a great
sign hanging over the road, to warn the approaching motorist
that there is a traffic light ahead; and about a hundred yards
nearer there is another warning, this one in the form of a
standard with an arm reaching over the road and a flickering
yellow light at the end of the arm. Then there are the traffic
lights proper—there is one light on each side of the road and
two more hanging over it. They have to have all the warnings
and lights, for the traffic that moves three or four abreast in both
directions is travelling at anything up to ninety miles an hour.
The cars hurtle past with a steady slap-slap-slap against the
joints of the concrete slabs of the road, and the trucks come up

with a great roar from their engines and a pounding from their
wheels that make the road shake beneath them. There is no
time to see the faces of the drivers as they pass; there is barely
time to see anything of the cars, except a headlight, a smear of
chromium, a curved window; and of each truck a jet of smoke
blown back from the funnel, before it is gone again with all its
weight swaying behind it, black tyres moving so fast they seem
to waver like something seen in water. And over on the opposite
side of the road, in the opposite direction, are other cars and
trucks, travelling at the same speed, also three or four abreast.
When the lights change they come slower, and we can see the
slower movement reaching back along the road, until all the
cars are at a standstill, and the smaller cross-stream enters the
road, swerves, and in a moment has accelerated to the left and
the right. And behind on the highway come other cars, moving
fast, but before they can reach the stationary cars the lights
have changed again, the cars have pulled away fiercely, and the
traffic on the Bayshore Highway is moving uninterruptedly
again, at the speed that the cars and the road (but for this
intersection, soon to be abolished) were built for.

That is the road. On the left of the road there is a tract of
houses, behind a single brown wooden fence running for hundreds of yards, and above the line of the fence there is the line of
the flat wooden roof-tops, every one at exactly the same height
as every other, end-on, and the same colour as the fence. Only
the poles rise above the roofs; and from every pole to the houses
within its reach there descends a multitude of wires, as if the
houses themselves are merely weights to keep the poles from
blowing away in the first strong wind. Nearer there is a filling-
station on the left, its emblem a great glass circle, illuminated in
red, hanging in mid-air. The filling-station gleams beneath
its emblem; beyond there is another tract of houses, behind
another wooden fence, with more poles, more wires. But a sign
at the intersection tells us: Menlo Park City Limit; and another
sign: You Are Entering Palo Alto. And on the right there is a
string of miscellaneous wooden hutments that a sign with a
downward pointing arrow describes briefly as: Roadside
Business.

Then, straight down the road is flat; but we can see that the
Bayshore Highway where we stand is soon to be transformed

into the Bayshore Highway as it should be. For high against the
sky there is a bridge all black and grey, but disturbed with
silvery glitters, quick, almost fish-like, where the cars pass across
it. You approach this bridge along swirls of concrete which
carry you up, circling in a loop high above the ground, and put
you on the bridge, and send you across the bridge, and then
bring you down, to join the Bayshore Highway at an angle so
acute that as you travel towards the highway you are moving
almost parallel to it. A sign warns you: Merging Traffic; and
the same sign warns those already on the road. But there is
room enough for all, and away you race, your car among all the
others, at the speed that the traffic behind forces upon you. And
you travel past all the other roadside businesses, tract-houses,
factories; and another bridge like a great black dream suspended rises before you, with all its attendant curving, uplifted,
or down-dropping roads, and beyond another sign warns you:
Merging Traffic. Behind fences there are flat wooden roofs, and
glimpses of flat tarred roads running between the houses, but
you are no longer in Palo Alto, you are in Redwood City, as you
realize when you see a sign that says: You Are Now Leaving
Redwood City, and another that says: You Are Entering San
Carlos. There will be other overpasses and underpasses and
bridges and skyways, other towns with other names to pass you
before you come to San Francisco.

There the six and eight lanes of traffic are flung high into
swathes of tar and concrete that dwarf any you have seen before,
that dwarf even the city beneath them, as you approach it, hills
and skyscrapers all shrunken under the roads. Road upon road
diverge and converge, and all are up in the air, as though it
were nothing that roads should be lifted on stilts high into the
air, and others lifted higher yet, sheering apart from one another
before going down like ribbons flung from a height, coiled and
lapped over one another. This is a fantasy, a dream of wielding
weight and mass as if they could be moulded between the
fingers, a dream of power given body, here, where all the roads
meet against the sky, and where there is no place for people,
and only the roofs of the cars flash above the concrete parapets.

It is a dream of power given body; but who wields the
power?

$\rightarrow\!\!\leftarrow$ 4 $\rightarrow\!\!\leftarrow$

BUYING A CAR, FINDING A HOUSE

HOUSE-HUNTING, as I have indicated, was for me much more than a metaphorical activity at the beginning of our stay in California. Grateful though we were for the temporary accommodation that had been found for us by the university authorities, it was not of a kind that allowed us to rest there for long. But no sooner did I set out to find a house than I found I simply couldn't manage even that without a car. We had lived in England for a couple of years and managed quite comfortably without one; but California was clearly a different country altogether. The distances were defeating for the pedestrian; and the situation with regard to public transport was simply hopeless. Because everyone had a car the buses ran rarely; and because the buses ran rarely, everyone who possibly could bought a car. The man without a car was caught in the middle of this circle, from where he was able to watch what buses there were going at infrequent and indeterminate intervals along routes that only the bus drivers seemed to know about. These buses were never occupied by more than three or four people, and the driver, whose air of boredom and disbelief in his own occupation could be seen from many yards away.

And quite apart from the distances involved in getting from one place to the next, walking was curiously uncomfortable for other reasons. First of all, when you walked in the suburbs the chances were there would be no one else in sight who was walking; and this in itself was enough to make you feel uncomfortable. Then, the pavements and the roads and the gardens were all on one flat level with one another, and the houses had no fences; so that when you walked you were not only singular, but totally exposed in your singularity. Householders working in their gardens stopped to watch you go, and people in the passing cars turned their heads to stare in surprise at you. And you had to walk briskly and look neither to the right nor to the left, to avoid giving the impression of being either a prowler or a Peeping Tom. For all those fenceless houses were open to your

c

gaze, but you could not take advantage of this; and you did not walk very often, not even for the exercise. I remember one evening walking home a couple of miles at rush-hour, along busy neighbourhood roads filled with cars taking their owners home after work. On that long walk at the busiest time of the day, I passed only *one* other pedestrian, and he—like a warning —was a man in shorts and sandals and a long black beard.

Incidentally, before coming to America I had often wondered how people lived in houses without fences: surely, I had thought, Americans weren't as friendly with one another to the degree that this seemed to indicate. After being in California for a few weeks I no longer wondered about it, nor did I ascribe the fenceless state of the houses to American friendliness only. The point of a fence is to keep passers-by off one's property; when no one ever passes by your property you can do away with the fence. Schoolchildren walked on the pavements, going to and from school; but hardly anyone else ever did: all the others travelled in their motor cars, at thirty or forty miles an hour, and many yards away on the bald flat width of the road. So what purpose would a fence have served?

As for walking along the El Camino or the Bayshore Highway—there is no point in even mentioning the possibility. El Camino had a pavement it is true (the Bayshore Highway did not even have that); but no natural landscape could have been nearly as discouraging to walk along as those roads, with all their distances and waste stretches and with all the cars that passed along them, each car coming so fiercely—a threat as it approached and a mockery as it left.

Clearly we had to have a car. Everyone said so too. 'You can't manage without a car here,' they said. 'You can pick up one pretty cheaply, you know.' They made it sound so easy I was ashamed to admit that I didn't know how one went about buying a car—people always underestimate the helplessness of the brand-new bewildered new-comer, who finds it difficult enough to get to his temporary lodgings from three blocks away, let alone do anything so much more hazardous as driving the distance. And I wanted a cheap car, a really cheap car. I had thought of something in the neighbourhood of a hundred dollars, but when I said this they frowned, they said you had to be careful if you went down that low (there was all the more reason to be careful if you went any higher, I couldn't help thinking); they said—and here my heart went into my boots—that at that price it was purely a matter of luck. Luck—the luck purely of the draw—has never been anything for me to rely on; and I felt this even more acutely when my requests for a reasonably honest car-dealer were met with such humorous remarks as, 'Now you're asking for something!'

I suppose I was asking for something—what I was secretly asking for was for someone who 'knew about cars' to lead me to one particular car among the many thousand cars on display in the open near-by. I hardly dared to enter the used-car lots by myself, they were so bizarre and circus-like, with their streamers and bunting and neon signs and banners and chalked and painted signs—and all their cars. The cars were all the circus that anyone could want: swollen, shining, puffed-up monsters of cars, all in different colours outside and inside; their interiors were like rooms, with their lounge seats and their radios; their steering-wheels looked as though they had been made out of jade and pewter and whalebone and other semi-precious substances; their dashboards looked like the things that jazz bands play in front of or. the films. And they all looked factory-new to me. It was nearly four years since I had been in a country where American cars were in free supply, so that the styles of the last four years were all equally unfamiliar. And there were so many styles, so many colours, so many cars, thousands and thousands of them, parked nose to bumper in great rows, platoons, phalanxes, armies of gleaming and curved metal and glass. 'Clean!' the signs all shouted, 'Clean!' These cars positively shone, they glittered, why tell me that they were clean?

This was no way to buy a car; but things moved as they always do; and one day I went with a friend, who knew no more about cars than I did, to inspect a two-hundred-dollar car that it had been arranged we should see. Mr Dickson—we had been told—was expecting us. We drove down El Camino Real and found him eventually in one of those wooden shacks behind one of the innumerable squadrons of cars, under the usual bunting and plastic whirligigs turning in the breeze. Mr Dickson was tall, dressed in a light-weight suit that shone like some kind of metal; he had the thin frame and the anxious lined face of a dyspeptic, but the tanned skin of an outdoor man. He was eager to please; he shook hands; he said, 'It sure is hot,' and guffawed suddenly—a surprisingly deep sound that matched neither his frame, nor his restless eyes, nor the smile through which the sound was uttered. He took us across the sand, between the cars, to the purple one we had come to see. 'She doesn't *look* so good,' he admitted. 'But that poke on the door doesn't mean a thing. Look, it opens, it closes,' he said, slamming the dented door. He guffawed again. 'If it wasn't for that poke in the ribs there we'd be asking three hundred for her. But that doesn't mean she can't run. Get in, try her, look around, take your time, make up your mind.' His patter was exhausted; he attempted to revive himself with the deepest and most sepulchral guffaw we had yet heard from him. He failed; and withdrew with a kind of listless tact to one side, leaving us to look around.

Tact was called for, for neither of us had much idea of what we should look for. I opened the hood and my friend and I both stared inside, and then I closed the hood. We opened and closed all the doors. We switched on the lights and switched them off again. We started the car and drove it around the lot; we revved the engine; we brought it back to where Mr Dickson stood on the sand, his figure casting a lean shadow in front of him; and I saw at least how he got his tan.

We were back later that afternoon—my feeling about El Camino Real was such that I was almost surprised that we had managed to find the place again, that it was still there, that Mr Dickson was still there, that Mr Dickson recognized us. When I had signed the deed of sale Mr Dickson took it from me and looked carefully at the signature. 'You won't regret it,' he said. 'You've bought a good car, Don.'

Friends in England had written to me asking 'What's it really like in California?' Until a used-car salesman in a lot somewhere along El Camino has called you by what he imagines is your first name—I wanted to write back proudly, after I had bought the car—you have no idea *what* California is like.

After almost a year in California I am able to add at least that Mr Dickson was right about the car, if not about my name. It was a good car, and took us everywhere we wanted to go;

and when we left we sold it to a friend who writes that it is still going. And I suppose the best intimation of what it's like in California remains the fact that we were forced to buy a car even before we were able to start looking around for a place to live in.

It was not only house-hunting that became possible after I had bought the car. To have a car in California was not to surrender to the mechanization around one, but rather to take the first step towards mastering it. The distances immediately became manageable; social communication became possible; some of the habits of the people became understandable—buying a car, driving a car was altogether to become more human, not less so. One no longer felt dwarfed, clumsy, out of place; if no better place offered it was always possible to join the streams of cars going up and down the highway. There was a feeling of sheer relief in the acquisition of that car that I had never felt before, and have never felt since, on making any purchase. Usually, no matter how much enjoyment one hopes to get from a new possession one feels even in the act of acquiring it that one has taken on another burden, another weight. I felt nothing of this with the car, though heaven knows it was a weighty enough, four-doored, hundred-horsepowered object.

Still, even with the car, it was very difficult getting a place to live in: I did not need to read the newspapers to know that the Bay Area of California was enjoying a fantastic boom in population. 'It's those aircraft plants,' people said. 'They're moving into the district and they're just snapping up everything.' 'It's those electronic plants,' people said. 'They send scouts ahead, and they just grab everything that's going.' 'It's the schools,' they said. 'The year starts at the colleges, and wham! everything's gone.' The university housing office had nothing at the rent I could afford to pay; nor did the daily newspaper's 'Furnished Apartments' column; I failed to find anything by simply driving about along the streets of the towns and watching out for 'To Let' notices. There were real-estate agents in shacks along the roadsides, in hutments, in wooden pre-fabs, at the top of stairs in duplex apartments, on little islands of grass and sand where four roads met, in the half-deserted main streets of the towns, in the mammoth

shopping centres: and I went to them all; but none of them
seemed to have anything to offer.

When I did eventually find a place it was through an agent
in whom I had had so little confidence that even though he
asked me to call back—which none of the others had done—I
did not. This real-estate agent had a squashed, middle-aged,
gangsterish face, wore a violently blue suit, and told me that he
was interested in what he insisted on calling my 'case' because
he was a student himself. But my lack of confidence arose
fundamentally from the fact that his card and the sign in his
window described him as a 'Realtor and Sociologic Adviser'—a
combination of which I could make little, and felt I should
expect less.

But the day after I had seen him, there was a knock at the
door, and a rather suspicious but impressed landlady told me
that there was a man at the door who wanted to see me. When
I saw Mr La Visse—for that, let us say, was the agent's name,
Henry La Visse—I understood why the landlady was impressed.
Mr La Visse still wore his electric-blue suit, and now had also a
hat of precisely the same shade to match it. He wore his hat
tilted far back from his pale brow; as if to balance this, there
protruded from his lips a very large cigar. It was late afternoon,
and in the soft light of the setting sun Mr La Visse stood out
startlingly. He removed neither his hat nor his cigar, but said
accusingly to me: 'You let me down. You said you'd call.'

'No, I'm sorry, I was busy.'

'Too busy!' Mr La Visse stared at me. 'Listen, do you or
don't you want to rent a house?'

'I do.'

'Well, I've got one for you. A hundred dollars a month,
partly furnished. And brother, you better take it quick. I can
fill that place twenty times before the week-end. It's just that
you're a student, I thought I'd give you first chance,' he said,
and added, as if challenging me to deny the claim, 'being a
student myself. So let's go and see it.'

There was some scurrying back and forth while we got the
history student and his wife to baby-sit for us; when all the
arrangements were made Mr La Visse led my wife and me to
the largest car in this land of enormous cars that I had yet had
the opportunity of driving in. It was a Chrysler station-wagon;

there seemed to be room in it for several families and all their baggage; its colours on the exterior were black with pink door-panels; its interior was black and pink along the dashboard, and all leopard-skin on the seats. It was altogether a preposterous car. It had no clutch; there was a pedal which started it, and next to that pedal a broad bar, which as we drove Mr La Visse told me was a power-brake. 'And when I press that power-brake, you go through the window,' he said proudly.

I told him that I thought his car remarkable in every way. 'Well,' he said, 'that's what we Americans like. You'll learn what we like. Power! Speed! Size! That's what we want, and that's what we get.'

'You've certainly got them in this car.'

'I sure have. And if I didn't, you know what I'd do with this car?'

'No,' I said.

'*I'd dump it.* See. That's what we Americans are like. If it hasn't got it, *we dump it.*'

I shall write about the house later; at the moment all that needs to be said is that it was clean, pleasant, bigger than we had expected, sparsely furnished. Mr La Visse took us through it at top speed, saying every now and again, 'You've got to make up your minds. It's going, gone.' He snapped his fingers. In the bathroom he doused his cigar in the lavatory pan and then flushed it. 'See, it works,' he said, as the cigar butt swirled in the water and disappeared. After our experience at the boarding-house we were glad to see it.

My wife asked about china: we had none with us, and had hoped that it would be included in the furnishings.

'What do you mean, china? Plates, cups, saucers? You leave that to me, I'll fix you up.'

I said that I thought we'd take the place.

'Think? Think? You got to do better than that. Will you sign the lease?'

'Yes.'

'Then you move in tomorrow. You come to the office, you'll sign the contract, we'll drive to my place, and I'll give you plates and cups and saucers, and the place is all yours.' And we drove back to our lodgings at high speed.

The next day I signed the contract, and then followed his car in mine to his house, where he took me into the garage. The garage was filled—as were so many others we were to see—with an old refrigerator, a vacuum cleaner, a child's scooter, all kinds of similar discarded and expensive objects, and several boxes, one of which contained the china. 'This stuff,' Mr La Visse told me, 'comes from the Military Academy. And what those kids can't break, *nobody* can break.' The cups and plates and saucers were white, monstrously thick; and it is true that we didn't break a single one of them while we had them. 'Take it brother, it's yours.'

'How much will it be?' I asked.

Mr La Visse's eyes were a very light, flat blue, and I saw them looking at me in reproach. 'When Henry La Visse gives anything,' he told me, 'he *gives* it.'

'Thank you, Mr La Visse.'

'You just give it to another student when you leave, and I'll be happy.'

'I will, Mr La Visse.'

We walked through his front garden to the gate. 'Your wife like figs?' he asked me. He put his fingers to his mouth and whistled, and a small boy with a large face remarkably like his father's, came out of the house.

'Hi, Pop,' the small boy said.

'You get up that tree,' his father said sternly, pointing, 'and you pick a sack of figs.'

'Sure, Pop.'

I waited with Mr La Visse while the boy fetched a paper-bag, and then climbed up the fig-tree. He disappeared from sight; we heard twigs snapping and leaves shaking, and then the boy's voice, 'Say, Pop, how much is he paying you for all this?'

The features of Mr La Visse's face seemed to retreat within themselves for a moment, as if a hand had come flat against it. But then his features filled out again. He turned to me proudly. 'Do you hear that? That kid's no Communist. He's a real American boy!' He threw back his head and shouted at the boy, 'I'm *giving* them, can't you understand? Money isn't everything, you dope.'

'Sure, Pop. If you say so, Pop,' came the reply from the tree.

When the landlady heard that we were moving away, she said

that she would have the law on me. She claimed that the university had told her that I would be staying in the house for the full period of my fellowship, and demanded from me the rent she had lost through turning away innumerable college boys who had wanted to lease the rooms. As the only two college boys who had inspected the rooms while we were there had been heard by my wife to say, as they returned to their convertible parked beneath our window, 'I wouldn't stay there if you paid me the rent she's asking'—I didn't believe a word of this claim. I knew further that in taking the rooms for me the people at the university had repeatedly told the landlady that the arrangement was purely a stop-gap one; and I had told her the same thing without arousing any protest. I pointed all this out to her, and she suddenly abandoned her claims for sums over and above our lodging, but consoled herself by naming a wildly exorbitant figure for that.

We had this conversation in the dining-room—I suppose that was what the room could be called, though no one ever dined in it. The house had no rooms of the usual description at all. There was no lounge or living-room, everybody ate in the kitchen, the television set was in the hall, the biggest single piece of furniture in what I've called the dining-room was a large business-desk; but the upstairs landing was equipped with a sofa and racks of magazines laid out like in a doctor's waiting-room. Our bedrooms were unspeakable.

I offered her exactly one half of the figure she had named, though I felt that even that was too much. She refused to take it. I raised my figure by five dollars; she refused to take that. We were at an impasse. I would not go any higher; she would not come any lower; and neither of us had the law on our side, because no figure had ever been agreed upon. (Whenever I had raised the topic she had been too busy or too friendly to answer me.) Now I stood at the desk; she sat at the table, a little way off, and read the newspaper, ignoring me, snubbing me, making me feel bad—which I must admit I did. I said nothing; she said nothing; her newspaper crackled and the television boomed away in the hall. I repeated my last figure; but she stared steadfastly at her newspaper. So I took out my cheque-book and began to write a cheque for the last figure I had given. When I looked up, the newspaper had disappeared and the landlady was eyeing me as if the cheque were a gun in my hand, and she were making her last speech on earth. 'You must do what you believe to be right,' she said. 'I leave it to your conscience.' I put the cheque on the table. She took it, read it carefully, and shook her head, her worst fears confirmed. 'There's no way of telling with some people,' she told me, 'until you've had dealings with them.' 'That's quite true,' I said as sincerely as she.

But once she had put the cheque away she became very friendly again; she told me that just where we were going to live they were planning to build a clover-leaf junction with the Bayshore Highway. They were going to take the roof off our heads, she told me; but when they did we must remember that she'd be glad to have us all back. She also offered to lend me tables, chairs, and bedspreads from the store of these things that she had in her cellar.

I was so surprised at her warnings and her friendliness, that I thanked her effusively for them both. But they never did begin work on that clover-leaf junction, and we lived very comfortably for our time in California in the house that Mr La Visse had found for us. And when we left we handed on his cups and plates and saucers, as he had asked. But I must confess we had quite a job finding anyone—even among the graduate students we knew—who would take them.

✣ 5 ✣

ALL SHOOK UP

So IN WHAT was really a very short time we had a house and a car; but our troubles weren't over yet. In a sense they seemed to have just begun. On our very first morning in the house an elderly balding gentleman came to the door to offer me a subscription to the San Francisco *Chronicle*: though I had never seen him before, he knew my name, and knew that we had just moved into the house; and he assured me that if we undertook to buy the San Francisco *Chronicle* for not less than six months he would be happy to present me with a copy of Hammond's Atlas of the World as my 'premium'. I agreed to take the San Francisco *Chronicle* for not less than six months, and signed a little form to that effect, whereupon he walked back to his car, opened the boot, and presented me with a copy of Hammond's Atlas of the World.

This gentleman left us; he was followed by a lady who offered my wife a range of cosmetics packed in an elegant pale blue little suitcase. Then came another woman, who took photographs of children, and told us we could have a free studio portrait of the children if we would buy not less than three copies of the portrait to send away to family and friends. Someone phoned up on behalf of the Palo Alto *Times*; and someone else on behalf of the San Francisco *Examiner*. The postman called at about eleven in the morning; and left with us a brochure from a local drugstore, and a four-page advertisement in large newspaper format announcing the imminent arrival of 'Ward's Week'. The milkman—whose name was worked in red thread on the lapel of his spotless white overalls —left us an entire compendium of plastic instructions which we could thrust into the empty milk bottles when we put them outside. We also had a mysterious and indignant phone-call from a woman who asked me how much I was paying in rent. When I refused to tell her she said threateningly, 'I'll find out, you wait and see,' and then rang off. (Much later I told the

landlord about this call, and he replied, without indignation or
surprise, 'That'll be my crazy sister-in-law.')

We were left in peace for a while; and we spent the time
examining what we could buy in Ward's Week. (This—needless
to say—was only one of the innumerable Weeks we lived
through in California. We had, among others, Dairy Week,
and Linen Week, and Spaghetti Week. There were also some
Months, and many Days. Once I was given a single daffodil by
a whole troupe of pretty girls who were wheeling a barrow of
daffodils down University Avenue. I accepted the daffodil, but
asked the girls why they had given it to me. 'Oh,' they replied,
as if explaining everything, 'it's Daffodil Day!' and then went
off with their barrow.) The most important result of our
perusal of the Ward's Week advertisement was the purchase of
a small white radio for $14.50.

Immediately any sense of security that we might have been
developing was fractured into pieces and carried away into the
air, that in our innocence we had not known to be humming all
the time with innumerable maniac voices. The little white box
that we had bought for $14.50 brought all the voices together
in the space of the tuning-band, and sprayed them incessantly
out of the corner of the room: we did not have the strength to
turn the machine off. I have no idea how many different
transmitters there were available to us; and all of them seemed
to be on all day and all night: but none of them seemed to have
radio programmes—as we knew programmes—they simply
played a record and screamed a commercial, played a record
and screamed a commercial. So it seemed at first: later we
found that there were a few soap-operas in the mornings on
some stations, an occasional church service, and a quiz or two;
there were even one or two 'serious' programmes, we found,
on Sunday mornings. Later still we learned too to distinguish
between the kind of records and the kind of commercials that
some of the stations played. Thus there was one that played only
'Western-style' music—from morning to night there was nothing on this station but scraping violins and Hollywood cowboys
yodelling; the announcers too were 'Western-style', and always
said 'Howdy-folks'; 'Why don't you-all . . .' was their standard
introduction to a commercial. There was a station that went in
for cool jazz, and the announcers here all had smooth voices

and spoke through half-closed mouths, and never spoke of anyone but he was a 'cat' and never made an exclamation but it was 'Man!' There were stations that in the evenings broadcast only in Italian, Spanish, Chinese, Japanese; there were others that gave themselves over to evangelists of the most surprising denominations: I recall particularly a hoarse Russian Jew trying to convert his fellow-Jews to his own brand of Christianity, and a Baptist who in his sermon offered you a fountain-pen with the Lord's Prayer engraved on it for only $1.50. And there were stations that played classical music (*Claire de Lune* and selections from Bizet's *Carmen* especially) every evening. Of the rest of the entertainments from the rest of the stations I shall say more later—of the hit-parades, tops of the pops, Bay Area Favourites, Peninsula Picks; but it was not to these, nor to evangelists nor the cool cats nor the Chinese that we really listened at first. Our attention was all upon the commercials.

All Shook Up was one of Elvis Presley's most popular songs at the time we were listening; and all shook up was how I felt after the first few days of intensive listening to the commercials. They were worse than the records, worse than anything I had yet heard or seen in California. They were of a wild absurdity and mendacity that passed beyond belief; and at first we could hear nothing but the commercials, think of nothing but the commercials, despair about nothing as we despaired about the commercials. Their insistence, their silliness, their loudness, their fierceness, the energy that went into them—all shook up, indeed: I was all shook up; but so was the whole country to which I had come, shaken into fragments that madmen held in hatfuls in their hands and pulled out and bawled at the tops of their voices, above massed brass bands and comic children and talking macaws and the sounds of bread being munched, potato chips being crunched, beer being drunk, drunks being punched, women coughing, gasping, sneezing, screaming, while the voices still sang, cajoled, pleaded, implored, commanded, insinuated, insisted without pause, as the fragments were shaken up and pulled out again.

Language and voice and manner and tune and style were all ransacked. There was no form of expression that was not broken and twisted before being used; and if there was no aspect of the country that was not involved and exploited and abused, there was also none that did not lend itself to abuse and exploitation. The military might of the United States was a trumpet and six female voices singing:

> To be strong in the air
> We need MEN
> In the Air Force;

and Government itself was the Republican Party buying time for a single voice to sing in the do-re-mi scale just: 'Vote, vote, vote, vote, vote, vote, vote, vote.' Finance was a barbershop quartet singing:

> Whatever your business
> Whatever you do
> First National is the bank-for-you.

Industry and Commerce were just a crazy babble of voices; High Culture an unctuous voice breaking into the *Nutcracker Suite* with an appeal to buy beer or furniture or more High Culture in the form of a long-playing record of the *Nutcracker Suite*. . . .

But who was there who didn't buy time to peddle his wares? The radio stations peddled themselves frantically: every now and again we would be urgently reminded, 'You are listening to KOBY, survey-proven the most-listened-to station in the entire Bay Area'; or the voices would sing:

> In San Francisco
> Everyone every day
> Listens to KYA
> THE PERSONALITY STATION

or desperate voices would urge a local patriotism upon the listeners: 'This is the *only* radio station in the south-central San Joaquin area—so you folks in the south-central San Joaquin area, you'll keep us tuned, won't you? Won't you? Please!' When the time for the news came around someone might sing:

> Keep informed, dial us in
> That's all you have to do.
> Every hour, five minutes up,
> We bring the news to you.

or we would hear the chatter of a ticker-tape growing louder and louder, followed by some kind of dramatic explosion, above which a voice would cry, 'We spotlight the globe!' and the news would follow, each item being followed and preceded by more ticker-tape noises, more explosions, and more cries of, 'We spotlight the globe!'

A toystore just up the road from ourselves bought time to announce the imminent arrival of a shipment of fur monkeys ('with washable nylon paws!'); a drive-in announced its special steak-dish twenty or thirty times in a single day on several stations ('and if you can't finish one of our steaks, why, you take what's left in a special hygienic cardboard container which we provide, and you give it to your dog. He'll love it!'); innumerable used-car merchants announced their daily snips ('and here we have a 1950 Chevvie station-wagon, heater and radio, cream panelling, for only $300. What? A 1950 Chevvie station-wagon with heater and radio and cream panelling for only $300? Yes, sirree, that's what I said.'); dentists announced a complete set of dentures for only $30 ('. . . *and* there's no down-payment folks. With dentures from Dr Snout's surgery you pay as you chew!'); magazines announced their future articles ('. . . have you ever wondered what it is like to lose a baby? Read the compassionate, heartwarming story of the mother who lost *her* baby, in the latest issue of . . .').

But really there is no way of conveying what it was like, except for a tape-recording of an hour's listening on about half a dozen stations, prefaced and followed and repeatedly punctuated with the warning that all of that and very much more went on all the time, week-day and week-end, day and night, with never a moment's pause; and that all this outpouring was no more than a part of what was produced in a single small corner of the states of the forty-eight. Behind us was the country we had flown over: plains, mountains, great industrial cities, big towns, small towns, villages, each with its own stations announcing its own items in its own used-car lots, drugstores, supermarkets, hardware shops—wares being peddled and peddled with a relentless, frightening, ever-new, unappeasable energy, and each station at the same time peddling itself too. The time and the money and the talent and the ingenuity that was flung into the air, the wealth that was squandered to maintain it all, and the uprooted semi-nomadic people living in a world of cheapjack goods around us which all this presupposed— here seemed to be matter to make one despair and despair again.

And it was of little comfort to reflect that the radio mattered so much less than it had once done as a medium of communication, that it was a comparatively shabby, neglected, all-but discarded medium, that people used it only to wake themselves up or to keep themselves awake while they were driving in their cars, or as a background noise to their business or household activities. (Incidentally, to judge from the number of commercials that were directed at car-drivers while they were driving, it is on car radios that the radio industry has come to lean most heavily for its market. In this case, the market, though smaller than it once was, remains assured, because everyone has a car but no one can possibly watch television while he drives it.) But if all we heard was what these people did when the medium was of little importance, what on earth would they do when the medium was of great importance?

Unfortunately I didn't have much chance to watch television when I was in California; but what I saw was not encouraging. It was true that there were programmes on television in a way that there no longer seemed to be programmes on the radio; but these programmes were interrupted often enough by the commercials; and it would be grossly untrue to say that the programmes anyway were generally of a high quality, or even frequently of a high quality, or even occasionally of a high quality. And though there were fewer commercials, by and large, on television than there were on the radio, the fact is that television, simply by its nature, is a more powerful and effective medium than radio; and one commercial on the television displayed as much absurdity and caused as much embarrassment as three or four or even half a dozen on the radio. It was very simple. On television one saw as well as heard the unfortunate people who sang and danced and pleaded in the name of deodorants and breakfast foods : one saw the comic children squeezing the bread between their fingers ('Oh Marm, it's squee-e-e-e-zing fresh!'), the penguins, cows, ducks, chimpanzees—whole zoos and aviaries and kindergartens performing their tricks for the advertisers, not to mention the adults, with their winking and leering and grinning and ultimate, inevitable, inescapable maddening naming of names.

I don't think it is possible to over-estimate the effect that the sight and sound of the advertising in America has on the newcomer; nor, however, do I think any warning can prepare the visitor against what he will find. The huge billboards illumined with floodlights and the neon signs that we saw on our first drive in California were merely the beginning of something that seemed to have no end. There was the radio; there was the television; there were the newspapers and magazines; there were the hundreds of brochures, leaflets, and announcements that were brought into the house—whether we wanted them or not—by the postman; there were the salesmen who called on the telephone or came personally to the door. Wherever we went, wherever we turned, there were the advertisements and the advertisers. Every medium of communication —including the roads—was physically dominated by the advertisements of a loudness and vulgarity that cannot be caricatured by exaggeration, because they were so much louder and more vulgar than the wildest exaggeration that anyone would dare to imagine.

And this—it must seem to the newcomer—is the voice and the face of America. This is what America sees when it looks into the mirror; this is what America hears when it talks to itself. If the Americans were determined to convince a visitor that individually and collectively they are a nation of infinitely manipulable morons and idiots—lost to all reason, without manners or ideas, devoid of even the crudest aesthetic sense, victims and users of a totally debased language—a nation whose style is a grossness and whose tone a loudness—if, as I say, that is the impression the Americans want to make on a visitor, then they really have cause to be grateful to their advertisers.

And there are not only the advertisements that achieve a success of this kind: the advertisements are, after all, only one feature of the mass-media of communication that in America seem at first to the newcomer to be more powerful, to have a larger audience and to be more certain of their audience than anywhere else in the world. This 'seem' is not a simple one, as I

D

hope to show; but it is appearances, likelihoods, first impres-
sions that I am dealing with now, and the appearances all
pointed to the unqualified and unassailable power of the mass-
media in American life—their power to mould taste and
opinion in every sphere of the life of the group and the individual.

Take the music that came over the radio—the pops, the hits,
the picks. (None of them lasted for more than a few weeks: once
they had been hit, picked and popped they dropped out of sight
like something down a mine-shaft.) They were all noisy, with
asinine or suggestive lyrics sung by weird-voiced vocalists or
played by great desperate bands of saxophonists and trum-
peters; but what was really bad about them—it seemed to me
—was that they were so damned good at their job. If you
wanted a loud, rhythmic and desperate noise in your ears, these
people gave it to you, week after week, day after day, more
loudly, more rhythmically, and more desperately than anyone
else in the world. Elvis Presley did with all his different voices—
the standard brazen, the coaxing husky, the sudden yelling, the
squeezed-out whimpering. Johnnie Ray did it by simply howl-
ing out his anguish, as if no pain before had been like his. Tab
Hunter did it bashfully; Pat Boone did it happy-go-luckily;
Patience and Prudence did it with voices as suggestively chaste
as their names; and so did all the others, so many others.
They sang for money, they sang for fame; but it was obvious, if
one listened to them, that they sang for love too.

True, the lyrics were machine-made, the tunes were repetitive and coarse, easily arrived-at, the singers did their tricks in
record after record, striving to reproduce each time—with just
sufficient a variation to keep the interest of their public—
whatever gimmick of voice or accent or manner had brought
them as far as they had come. Yet, unmistakably, to these
people the world they inhabited was in some way a real world,
and the kings and queens among them were real kings and
queens. The rewards of royalty were great, could be seen in
every newspaper, on the covers of innumerable publications
devoted to their life-stories, or simply—as I saw one series—to
their Moods (with a different photograph of each Mood).
Behind and in front of every one of these performers was this
world of celebrity and wealth—our world too, whether we live

in America or England or South Africa. The tunes we heard in
California on our little white radio would be sung by Bantu
houseboys in Johannesburg; I have already heard several
whistled nearby along the be-hedged sunken lanes of Devon.
Terrible! Terrible! one feels one should say immediately, and
I suppose it is, and for more than one reason. Since coming
back to England I have listened to the English versions of
many of the hits I heard in California and these English
versions generally are poorer, thinner, quieter, weaker in every
way. But—so complex are these things—this does not make
them any the less terrible. It makes them more so.

But though they were so easily available—so difficult to
avoid, indeed—in California, one does not really need to go to
California to hear Elvis Presley or Johnnie Ray; so I shall say
no more here about them. Nor about the movies, which also
come to you wherever you live, or the fat multi-coloured
magazines, or the television quizzes, personality shows, the
fan-magazines, pin-up pictures, and all the rest. I will say only
that—familiar though I thought myself to be with all these
things, and all the rest of the devices, entertainments, bombardments of the American mass-culture—it was for me an extraordinary experience to feel the impact of the culture in a country
where *everything else* was American too. That—ultimately and
simply—was the extra dimension of the power that the mass-
media seemed to have acquired over me from the moment I
stepped on to American soil: for here only three hundred miles
from Hollywood, was the home, the origin, the birthplace of
the American mass-culture, the first and most thoroughly
subjugated territory of all.

THINGS

THE NEWER middle-class houses in Palo
towns went under many names and desc
descriptions including sooner or later
Living', 'Ranch Style', 'Californian', '
and Gracious', 'Suburban'. But there w
saw, though to me it seemed to describe th
the word 'Democratic'. And when I say
mean only the outside appearance of a
this I have already attempted to describe,
spectacle to see a thousand of these R
Living, Gracious and Spacious wooden b
one another in their uniform thousands. B
houses were democratic too, in a differen

We were in several tract-houses, and t
designs differed, in one thing they were al
in all was on open floor-space—in every
as wide-open to one another as they could
doors, and divisions as possible. Hence, to
were 'spacious'; hence they were built
hence, in my opinion, they were 'democ
walls and doors distinctions were done a
between hosts and guests, between par
some the attempt had even been bravely
the distinction between indoors and out
who lived together in these houses were
cook together in the living-room and to
to romp together in the rumpus room, a
together in the bedrooms. It was all un
friendly; almost the entire house and the
display all the time, as if none of the occ
would ever have anything to hide from o
the family parents would have nothin
children, children from parents, and hus
each other.

in America or England or South Africa. The tunes we heard in California on our little white radio would be sung by Bantu houseboys in Johannesburg; I have already heard several whistled nearby along the be-hedged sunken lanes of Devon. Terrible! Terrible! one feels one should say immediately, and I suppose it is, and for more than one reason. Since coming back to England I have listened to the English versions of many of the hits I heard in California and these English versions generally are poorer, thinner, quieter, weaker in every way. But—so complex are these things—this does not make them any the less terrible. It makes them more so.

But though they were so easily available—so difficult to avoid, indeed—in California, one does not really need to go to California to hear Elvis Presley or Johnnie Ray; so I shall say no more here about them. Nor about the movies, which also come to you wherever you live, or the fat multi-coloured magazines, or the television quizzes, personality shows, the fan-magazines, pin-up pictures, and all the rest. I will say only that—familiar though I thought myself to be with all these things, and all the rest of the devices, entertainments, bombardments of the American mass-culture—it was for me an extraordinary experience to feel the impact of the culture in a country where *everything else* was American too. That—ultimately and simply—was the extra dimension of the power that the mass-media seemed to have acquired over me from the moment I stepped on to American soil: for here only three hundred miles from Hollywood, was the home, the origin, the birthplace of the American mass-culture, the first and most thoroughly subjugated territory of all.

6

THINGS

THE NEWER middle-class houses in Palo Alto and the other towns went under many names and descriptions, most of the descriptions including sooner or later words like 'Family Living', 'Ranch Style', 'Californian', 'Outdoors', 'Spacious and Gracious', 'Suburban'. But there was one word I never saw, though to me it seemed to describe them most accurately— the word 'Democratic'. And when I say democratic I do not mean only the outside appearance of a mass of these houses: this I have already attempted to describe, and it is a lamentable spectacle to see a thousand of these Ranch Style, Family Living, Gracious and Spacious wooden boxes squatting behind one another in their uniform thousands. But the interiors of the houses were democratic too, in a different way.

We were in several tract-houses, and though the individual designs differed, in one thing they were all alike. The emphasis in all was on open floor-space—in every house the rooms were as wide-open to one another as they could be, with as few walls, doors, and divisions as possible. Hence, to the copywriters, they were 'spacious'; hence they were built for 'family living'; hence, in my opinion, they were 'democratic'. By abolishing walls and doors distinctions were done away with—distinctions between hosts and guests, between parents and children; in some the attempt had even been bravely made to do away with the distinction between indoors and outdoors. And the people who lived together in these houses were obviously expected to cook together in the living-room and to eat together there too, to romp together in the rumpus room, and practically to sleep together in the bedrooms. It was all unmistakably open and friendly; almost the entire house and the entire family were on display all the time, as if none of the occupants of these houses would ever have anything to hide from outsiders, just as within the family parents would have nothing to hide from their children, children from parents, and husbands and wives from each other.

This arrangement—or suggested arrangement—seemed to me at least as new and surprising as the equipment with which each house was provided. But before detailing some of the items of this equipment, I should emphasize that the homes I am describing were not at all for wealthy folk: they were intended rather for what one may call the sub-professional classes, those who do less well out of their professions than, say, doctors, or architects. We knew several university lecturers who lived in houses like these, a teacher at a junior school, a man who was an assistant at a furniture store, a reporter on a local newspaper, a psychologist employed by a research institute. They were all young people who had just started their careers and had put down something on their house and were paying the rest off. And it was taken for granted that people of this class should be able to move into homes that were ready-equipped with *all* of the following: a large electric stove, a large refrigerator, a large washing-machine, a large tumbler-dryer, and a furnace that heated the entire house as a thermostat dictated; most of the houses had garbage disposers and water-softening machines as well. Television sets, radios that woke you up and made your coffee at the same time, hi-fi gramophones and mixmasters you presumably had to provide yourself, if you wanted them, and a great many people did; but even without the extras each of these mass-produced, middle-class, matchbox homes looked opulent enough, once you were inside them. There was no escaping 'Contemporary' or 'Scandinavian' furniture anywhere you went; and there was not a little back lawn that was not equipped with swings for the children and a barbecue on wheels for the grown-ups.

The equipment of a middle-class household in Palo Alto, and the staggering size and numbers of the cars that were on the roads were just a part of the over-all air of prosperity, of opulence indeed, that is quite unlike anything I have ever seen anywhere else in the world. In fact, it is possible to see it nowhere else in the world but in America—and in America, of all states, most in California; and in California as much in the Bay Area suburban towns as anywhere else. I remember reading somewhere that the average income in the Palo Alto area was about fifteen per cent—if I remember rightly—above the

average income in the State of California; and the average
income in the State of California is, I imagine, somewhat
higher than the national average. But even if one were to
imagine the same number of people in Palo Alto, and subtract
twenty or thirty per cent of their possessions, they would still
have been remarkably prosperous, by any standards.

It was impossible not to be dazzled by the glitter and the
profusion of goods that were on display in the shops and in the
homes, on the roads, that were stacked away carelessly in
garages or thrown away to rust in vacant lots, that were given
to children at school, that were thrust at one everywhere, all
the time. There was a constant massive creation, consumption
and disposal of goods—a sheer bulk of *things*—that we could no
more have imagined before coming to California than we could
have imagined the fierce, inescapable, nagging, maddening
persistence of the advertisements that were intended to hasten
the process.

The 'atmosphere' of life in Palo Alto was thus very much a
tangible affair, it was so much involved with the things we
found ourselves surrounded by. And these things were in
general big things—even the smaller things were bigger than
they would have been anywhere else, if I can express myself
that way. For instance, a drying-rack for plates in California
was at least one and a half times the size of the largest drying-
rack for plates that I had ever seen before; a packet of potato
chips was like a balloon blown out (the chips themselves were
almost palm-size); detergents came in great pails. What
wasn't King Size, in short, was Giant Size; and if it wasn't
Giant Size it was Family Size; and if it wasn't Family Size it
was nothing less than Jumbo Size. The American motor car
seemed to have set the style for American packaging in general
—everything, like the cars, came in a package that was glittering, inflated just beyond reasonable proportions into some
kind of mild fantasy object. The packaging was absurd and
often ugly; but it was in itself an indication of the grossest
prosperity. Only a country that had practically solved the
problem of production and was now faced with the problem of
what next to produce could possibly have spent so much money
on packaging. I still have with me a plastic potato-bag, which
we used as a bag for carrying children's toys in. This potato-bag

is big, of course, and is decorated with red, white, and blue stripes, and has a little transparent panel through which you can see the condition of the potatoes you are buying; on the back of the bag, also in red, white and blue, are stencilled four elaborate recipes for Potato Surprise, Potato Supreme, Potato Fritters, and Potato Potage, as well as a communication entitled 'Potato Know-How', which informs you that Waxy Potatoes are best for baking, broiling and frying, Mealy Potatoes are best for scalloping and creaming, and that to retain those valuable natural vitamins you should pare as closely as possible to the skin. It is altogether a remarkable potato-bag; and is illustrative of more, indeed, than prosperity and elaborate packaging.

With a packet of flour my wife received a palette knife; and with a packet of salt a 'jewel tumbler'; if you bought enough of one kind of margarine you could get a pair of silk stockings, and if you bought enough of another kind you could get a set of steak knives. Steak knives also came if you bought enough porridge, cake-mixes, and soap. The margarine, incidentally, never came but it was divided into four quarter-pound tablets individually wrapped in gleaming foil and then packaged together in a very large, highly decorated, grease-proofed, cardboard box. All that, and the promise of steak knives too. And the bread never came but it was ready-sliced and Totally Wrapped; and the milk never came but it was Homogenized and Vitamin-Enriched. Orange juice too was invariably homogenized; so was cream; so was yoghurt; so was peanut butter; so was dietetic milk for those who are slimming.

I had never felt the need for a special little metal brush to use for putting butter on corn on the cob when I ate corn on the cob; but there wasn't a hardware store in Palo Alto that wouldn't have been happy to provide me with a family-set of brushes for this very purpose. My wife had never noticed before how inconvenient it was that when she was finished using an oven-cloth she had to go and hang the oven-cloth on a hook; but in Palo Alto every supermarket had a special line of oven-cloths containing little magnets inserted in a corner of each, so that you could just fling the cloth against the side of the oven or any other metal surface, and it would stick there. Boys' jeans came with a built-in leather patch on the seat, so that from the day they're bought these jeans could look worn, old, rough, tough: and this leather, it should be added, was guaranteed laundry-proof. And that bitter taste that comes from licking the flaps of envelopes has been abolished in Palo Alto, where it was impossible to buy a packet of envelopes that did not have delicately spearmint-flavoured flaps. Such—one cannot resist saying—seemed to be the flavour of life in Palo Alto.

I suppose if one looks for them one can buy butter brushes for corn on the cob in London too, and spearmint-flavoured envelopes as well. The point was that in Palo Alto one didn't have to look for them. They were available everywhere. And the point too is that Palo Alto isn't London, but a town of about forty thousand people; and what Palo Alto had Redwood City had too, and San Jose had too, and Burlingame, and so too did every other of those towns along the highways.

But when one talks of Californian prosperity it is with the cars that one must end, just as it is with the cars that our awareness of it began. The number of cars that there were on the roads cannot be described, it can only be indicated weakly enough by saying that when a gang of roadmenders came to re-lay the tar in front of our house their cars were parked in a long string half-way down the block. And what the roadmenders had, the kind of family that I described in the beginning of this chapter had in double measure, for almost every garage of their homes was built for two and filled by two.

It had not been gracelessness and carelessness only that had sent these towns sprawling with all their waste spaces for car parks and their shopping centres alongside wide black roads that in themselves took up enough space for whole cities to be built. 'The trend,' as they said in every home-making journal that came out every month, 'is to suburban living'; but no one seemed to know quite where the trend would end. Already the hearts of the minor towns like Palo Alto had been sucked out by the highways and the shopping centres that serve them; and from the big cities one was beginning to hear the same complaint. And it all derived from the simple fact that the position has now been reached where practically every family has a motor car, and with a motor car it is possible to travel a mile in the same time that it would take you to walk a block.

The Americans themselves are surprised at this development,

and truly there is no one who knows where it will end. The name given to it is 'suburban' development; but to what 'urbs' are these places 'sub'? Not to one another, for they are all alike, all of much the same size, all dependent on the great main roads that run past them. Nor in a sense are they dependent on the big city near them, if there happens to be a big city near by. It is true that a great many of the suburbanites commuted every day to and from San Francisco; but the big firms themselves seemed to be abandoning San Francisco. Every big department store in San Francisco was represented by branches in the shopping centres along the highways, and factories were being built alongside the highways; there was even, I remember, the West Coast office of a big publishing firm somewhere along the highway.

What I had seen was new not only to me but to America too: it is not so very long that America has been prosperous enough to put a car into so many millions of garages; and there is no one who is not gaping in wonder and groping for reassurance now that he sees what the first result has been. The universal possession of the motor car has made it possible in California for the activities of modern industrial and urban life, which once had to be concentrated as closely as possible together, to be dispersed over tens and twenties and thirties of miles. It is an ironic thought that the same industrialism which was responsible for the sudden massive development of cities in every industrialized society in the world is now—in California at least—offering the first real threat to the predominance of the cities.

Everyone in America makes jokes about the suburbanites, with their barbecues in the back yard and their station-wagon in their garage; but they make jokes partly because they are frightened. We have never before had any kind of society— never before thought any kind of society possible—in which every member is able at will and in his own vehicle to cover a distance of sixty miles in as many minutes; and, what is more, in which every member of the society does so, frequently. They say that one day there is going to be a single 'town' (which will be no-town) stretching all the way from Los Angeles to San Francisco. But to understand this prospect is hardly to forgive it.

Part Two

FURTHER AFIELD

✦

7

SAN FRANCISCO TO YOSEMITE

A TRAVEL-BOOK should be about travelling; but I am afraid
that most of the travelling that we did has already been described. However, we did see a little more of California than
what lay beyond the string of towns in the Bay Area; and there
was San Francisco itself, which we visited several times. San
Francisco I had always thought of as a city right at the very end
of my world, and I had no sooner left than it became that again
—a place distant, almost unreal, remembered without conviction. Partly, I suspect, that is the fault of the city itself, for
though San Francisco is a city which more than most in
America is supposed to have a particular legendary quality,
and though it is dramatically enough situated—on the very edge
of the bay, with the two great and beautiful bridges flung out
like wings on either side—as a town it did not seem to me to
measure up in any significant way either to its situation or to its
own legend. It seemed, in fact, a mucky kind of a place, lacking
elegance and style, smeared all over with neon, dominated by
some tall buildings that were neither handsome nor distinctive,
surrounded by barrack-like suburbs of little square houses. It
was nothing more in short than another jumble—of a kind
different to the jumbles we had grown wearyingly familiar with
in the suburban towns, but a jumble nevertheless.

Continually one thought in San Francisco what this place
could have been like, with the hills crowning it, with the
mountains backing away from it to the south, with the water all
around it. And there was the history of the town—always told as
a series of disreputable days of cosmopolitan high living and
earthquakes and gold rushes. And Chinatown was charming
enough in its touristy way, and the Fisherman's Wharf was
charming in its touristy way, and the International Settlement
was charming in its sadly decayed and equally touristy way,
where the contrived ghosts of good times at the burlesque linger
among the cracked gilt and the coloured tiles and the pictures

of the legs of girls who'll dance no more. But one charm—such as it was—contributed to no other; the spirit sagged in the rubbishy grey streets between. Market Street particularly stands out in my mind as one of the ugliest main streets I have ever seen, so besmeared with signs over its buildings that there was nothing for the eye to do but dart from place to place in a vain search for a resting-place. The city, as a city, made no gesture, spoke no meaningful word. And it was so very anxious to: perhaps that was the trouble.

No, there was nothing in San Francisco that so became it as the ways along which one could approach or leave it. The first half of the Bay Bridge, before it dives through Treasure Island and re-emerges in a less graceful form on the other side—the first half of the Bay Bridge is one of the most superb human structures I have ever seen, or hope to see. It stands so high, it is so huge and grey, with all its steel and concrete and its wide and ever-busy lanes of traffic on two decks, like a whole city; and yet it travels so easily, with arcs suspending it so lightly as they rise to the towers and sink away, only to rise again. Golden Gate Bridge too had the same strength and lightness, the same purposefulness and ease; but it is the Bay Bridge that I most remember, perhaps because I had not been warned about it and it came as such a surprise.

And on the other side of Bay Bridge one came to a place where roads swooped up to the bridge and spiralled down from it, where the roads were woven over and under the bridge and each other—and all in the air!—as if there were nothing to marvel at that so many roads of such sizes should be up in the air. There were places like this on both sides of the bridge and again a little further out of San Francisco. To me they were a wonder every time I saw them; and I still don't understand why no one talks more of these astonishing structures. And structures like them stand outside every big American city.

Or one could leave San Francisco on the far side of the Golden Gate, and fall among bare hills of grass, the city behind one assuming some dignity and order the further one got from it, each of the thousand tall shoulders of concrete cut clean against the air. Or one could sail under the Bay Bridge, seeing from below how still it hung in the air; as the boat moved the glittering towers of the city seemed to move too, crowding closer and closer together, until in the distance they seemed all to have been struck from a single rock.

And southwards one could drive along the saddle of the Santa Cruz mountains, with reservoirs for the city in the valleys below, and green forests of pine and firs and coast redwoods standing upright against the slopes from which they grew, and glimpses of brown-grassed hills further off. Coming down on the east there was the brown plain of the Bay Area laid out flat below, with the dots and cubes of houses shining in glints against the paleness of the earth and the grey haze of the Bay Area smog. Westwards the mountains dropped down to the Pacific, the hills undulating towards the sea; every hill broken only by the sallow flattened humps of the liveoak trees.

On the foothills of the mountains were the houses of the rich, within easy reach of the suburban towns and the highways, yet set comfortably back from them. They were modern enough, these houses, many of them of bold and elaborate architecture, with split-levels and patios and carports and light timber beams exposed and flagged verandas outside glass doors that remained open through all the summer days and evenings. Yet somehow they did not seem attractive to live in, and I am still a little puzzled to know why; I think I would have preferred a house in one of the suburban towns, if I had to live in California permanently, rather than those houses perched on the hill-tops or set against the flanks of the mountains.

In the towns, I suppose, one was able pretty much to forget about the seasons, about natural California altogether. This forgetfulness was helped by the fact that the seasons in California were not really noticeable: the sun shone most of the year, and while it was true that we had rain in the winter and none in the summer, there was no snow, no really bitter cold; when spring came the grass turned green and some of the trees put on a few more leaves, and that was all; in summer the grass turned brown. These movements were all small; there was none of the slow and profound turning of the year that one has in other climates, and that penetrates the consciousness of even the most boxed-in city dweller in the blackest of cities. And then one's indifference to what lay beyond the highways and the drive-ins and the little wooden houses was encouraged too by

the fact that so very often one could not see beyond them,
anyway: hills and mountains and horizons were hidden often
by the smog that came creeping down the Bay Area, walling it
in, concentrating the light upon what glittered and flickered
near to hand. So sunk in the jumble, one was not reminded of
the failure of the Californians to come to terms with the country
that surrounded them. When the fog lifted, or when one was
visiting one of these houses in the foothills, the reminder was
always there.

It is difficult enough to talk about the relation of any people
to the country that surrounds them; but in California the
relationship which one felt seems even more difficult to describe
than is usually the case. In South Africa, for instance, there is
also a failure on the part of the country's inhabitants to come to
terms with the country in which they live. The cities are
dwarfed by the spaces and silences that surround them; in
Cape Town, in Kimberley, even in Johannesburg, one has just
to lift one's head to become aware so often of the thinness and
tenuousness of the relationship that the bold buildings and the
telegraph poles have to the naked and indifferent veld around
them. South Africans have just scratched the surface of their
country, which remains always beyond them, unassailable,
uninterpretable, always bigger and dryer and more imposing
than they are or what they do to it. There is pathos in the
relationship, a sense of loss and powerlessness.

And England again, is quite different. The people seem to
fit the country (what is left of the country, outside the cities)
and the country the people, so that one can hardly tell what is
natural and what man-made. Each at its best over the centuries
has become the other, in a congruence, a harmony of field and
house, road and hedge, wood and village, moor and harbour,
that is a continual surprise and reassurance to the spirit.

But in both South Africa and England there is this relationship, to be perceived and described. In California, however,
there seemed to be no congruence, as in England; nor was there
defeat and powerlessness, as in South Africa; powerlessness is
the last thing one would ascribe to the Californians. Their
towns and their houses are simply thrust down, ignoring,
making null and unnoticeable the country on which they are
built; and the country, for its part, seems to have nothing to

do with the towns and the houses that have been placed on it. There is an abruptness in the change from what is man-made and what is natural, an equality of powers that has produced merely a disjuncture and an indifference.

And this too is new: that men should have been powerful enough to do this, to seem to ignore in this way the land they settle in.

We left Palo Alto on one Sunday morning, and turned the car southwards on the Bayshore Highway. The road was crowded with Sunday traffic: all the weekday trucks were there, and all the private cars carrying their families to visit other families, and cars towing speedboats behind them, and cars with leather-jacketed boys towing motor bikes in trailers behind them, and stripped and numbered hot-rod cars, all pelting along the main road between San Francisco and Los Angeles, as if all week no one had been able to move and everyone was now moving as fast and as far as he possibly could in the one day given to him. We followed Highway 101 some way beyond San Jose, suburban town after town passing to the left and right; and then turned off into a side-road that was emptier, and that took us through the Pacheco Pass. On the other side of the Pass the hills were all green and silver, falling and rising in curves, covered only with the unstirring, silver-tipped grass that threw no shadow but lay in equal light everywhere, under the sun—the softest light and the least harsh country we saw anywhere in California.

In the San Joaquin Valley the light was dulled by dust, and the earth neither lifted nor dropped, and the road ran straight into the east like an arm pointing: only the silver water-tanks of each dusty and bedraggled and shadeless little township of wooden houses rose above the level of the plain. The tanks gleamed in the confused light: but all other colours were yellow and whitish. The flat fields had been cut, and only a stubble was left. The miles passed without distinction, like the townships lost behind us, and all the fields and wire fences running to the horizon at right angles from the road.

Then sluggish and black ahead of us we saw a main highway, with the traffic moving ant-like on it, and we came to the highway, and turned among the traffic, which once we were close to it was a continual roar and an intermittent thud and a

E

flashing of the sunlight against metal and glass. Sadder and dirtier and móre haphazard than on the roads near Palo Alto were all the drive-ins and filling-stations and motels, and shadeless too, no trees anywhere near the wide expanse of the highway or the jumbled occasional buildings alongside it or the fields that stretched away from it. Like a cataract moving in both directions the road poured through a place called Madera, but we stopped there for petrol, and as we stretched our legs we were able to feel the continual nerve-like shudder of the earth beneath our feet, as the traffic passed on the road.

And Madera has remained in the mind as the type of all those inland towns we passed through on our way to Yosemite and our way back again : a place without shade, laid down square in a grid that loses its shape on either side, where hot little cool-drink and hamburger stands and the motels string themselves out along the highway. Its central shopping area was a muck of buildings, of neon signs thrust close against one another and flickering against the fierce daylight—neither paint nor neon hiding anything of the clapboard shabbiness of the place, but only showing it up more crudely still. The sun blistered everything it touched, and there was nothing that it did not touch; there was nowhere to hide from it in Madera, or from the highway which drove wide through the town, with a noise like thunder and shaking of the earth, and swept on again, with all its width of tar and traffic. The forlornness of this place had nothing in common with the South African forlornness which I had known before : there was too much movement; too many people; too much metal, too much power to be forlorn in the South African way. Almost one might say that Madera was forlorn with an excess of power, were it not for the poverty and shabbiness of its frame buildings, and the harshness of the country that lay around it.

And as Madera was, so was Modesto, and Los Banos and so too were many of the places whose names we never learned but saw briefly from a car or a train in the United States—places of a barrenness and a harshness and an ugliness that was like an act of violence, an explosion of anger, a blow with a clenched fist, a pistol shot. The sense of violence done was inescapable : each place looked as though it had been flung down so hard that it cracked, and what was spattered furthest lay in the fragments of orange-juice stands and motel signs on the outskirts. Brutally, these places had nothing that was not for use: all that they were was exposed at a glance; they were without seclusion, without secrecy.

And indeed, one cannot come to the United States and travel about within it without developing a sense of violence having been done, and still being done, and even more dangerously impending. It is there in the dark, busy cities, with all their tall buildings and streets between; it is there on the roads that are built to carry the cars that rush like things gone amok; it is there in the raw and distant towns flung down like Madera for the selling of petrol, the canning of peas, the milling of lucerne, the housing of those who transact this business. Always, there is this sense of violence when one looks at the places that the people have put their hands to; towns so harsh and neon-lit and unpitied, so new, so restless with traffic and people who have the air always of having come from elsewhere. And one expects these people to be as harsh and unpitying as their cities and roads and towns; and there is, indeed, more violence in the United States than in a country like England; there are more murders, rapes, riots, lynchings, more sudden, savage and unpredictable outbreaks of rage and fear and frustration.

But when one *sees* a place like Modesto or Madera, the wonder is only that there is not more yet; and when one considers that most of these people do in fact come from elsewhere, and are new to their country, and that their loudest guides to conduct seem to be the advertisers and the radio and the television and the tabloid press, the wonder is that they aren't all continuously and desperately at war with one another, that there is so little frenzy, so few stabbings and acts of arson and bombing, that over a continent of towns like Modesto and even worse cities, there should be so much peace, so much gentleness.

We left the highway at Madera, and turned again into a side-road, that ran level for some time, and then started lifting, always lifting, to the mountains whose white peaks we could see far ahead of us. The grass gave way to wood, and liveoaks and cottonwood gave way to conifers, and soon we were driving through pine forests, every tree upright, straight-trunked, like a jet thrown up. And so the mountains went on, still higher, and now among all the darkness of tree trunks and the bristling of the pine needles, there lay white patches of snow disregarded on the ground. The peaks we had seen earlier no longer seemed to hang disconnected; but we could see the pine-covered slopes sweeping up towards each one and tumbling down from it, rock and pine and snow, each at rest where it stood, and all part of the wild upward surge.

We stopped at a place where there were two motels and a store and a creek that the road passed over on a bridge. The buildings were set on levels cut out of the slopes, where the trees had been felled, one slope ascending in shadow, the other in sunlight. But the shadow came soon enough on them both. We were the only guests at the motel, which was very new and clean; I walked down later to the other motel, which was also new and clean and empty, and had a drink at the bar there. The proprietors of this motel were a pair of brothers—extraordinary-looking young men, so tall that they had to bend their heads when they entered their own doors, with long thin faces and large eyes and small twisted mouths and dark skins. They looked like something remote—Abyssinians, Khazaks, something like that—but one played the juke-box and imitated Elvis Presley; the other stood behind the bar and admired his brother's display of talent; and a fat little man in blue overalls—the only customer—said that he couldn't stand Elvis Presley's singing but he sure admired the —— —— —— for making so much money.

The next morning we entered the Yosemite National Park. We were right out of season, and most of the park was closed; but what was open to us was as big as several English counties, and we gladly exchanged the area we couldn't visit for the advantage of having the park so much to ourselves. We stayed at one of the lodges in the Yosemite Valley, and I remember that when I came out of our cabin the first morning, I looked up at the granite wall nearest to me—and I looked up, and up, and up, involuntarily, unconsciously, looking for the end, and not finding it until my head was strained far back. And then only did I see the rim of the cliff, thousands of feet above me. The valley was narrower than seemed possible to support the weight and height of the walls that towered up so closely on both sides. And it seemed too small also to take the flow of the water that all day and all night, from twenty different points, fell from the cliffs in slender streams with such lightness and speed that it was almost frightening to see them, as if one feared the water could be hurt in its fall.

Beyond the granite walls were the Sierra Nevadas, white with snow, fanged with rock, slashed and cut by gorges and ravines and river-beds, crowned by peaks and the bold trees bristling. Spur and crest and ridge stood up across a waste of spurs and crests and ridges, with the high hidden valleys between; and what was not white was black—the trees, and the clefts in the rock, and the tiny birds that were the only things to be seen moving. Then we would go down to the valley again, away from the fierceness and desolation of the mountains to the archaic, impregnable shelter of granite, with its floor of grass.

But the shelter was not impregnable. A tribe of Indians had once lived in the Valley: the Yosemites they had called themselves, and they had been found by prospectors whose other finds had been marked with lying names like Coarsegold and El Dorado and Chinaman's Luck, on our way to Yosemite. As I remember the story, the Yosemite Indians had clashed with the prospectors, then with a team of Government surveyors, and then, and finally, with a detachment of the United States Army. That had been the end of the Yosemite Indians, who had been carted away to a reservation. Of them nothing remained but some photographs in the little museum near the lodge where we stayed, and a place called the Indian Camp, on the floor of the valley. Indian Camp was a few tumbled boulders and a few fissures in the granite wall, where a man could have hidden; the boulders were as big as rooms, and on the top of the flattest one of them a few holes had been scooped out of the rock. They were mortar holes, for grinding corn, pathetic little semi-artefacts filled now with dust and cigarette stubs.

The cars pulled up, their occupants climbed out, walked about among the boulders, peered doubtfully into the caves, had themselves photographed in front of the rock with the mortar-holes, and drove away again. Who would celebrate the dispossessed Yosemite Indians? What was there to celebrate? But who could celebrate the cars and the neat signposts pointing to the Indian Camp and the cameras that recorded the visit of

each party? It was impossible not to feel guilt before the mortar-
holes of these Yosemite Indians—guilt for their defeat, their
failure, the smallness of all they had managed to leave behind
them. Amid towering scenery in the shelter of their valley these
people had lived for who knew how long until they had been
driven out: and what a small ruin had they left. No Athens, no
Rome, no Jerusalem, not even a Zimbabwe had they managed
to build; and it was their powerlessness and simplicity that
made the guilt stronger, not less so.

Yet between those gigantic glacial walls, those who came in
their cars to be photographed with their children in front of
the boulders and then drive on again—they had their deep
pathos too. And this made it harder to patronize the Yosemite
Indians, who had tried their best, as these people were doing.
There is no way out of the struggle, for any of us.

Part Three

THE WILL AND THE WAY

→>—<←

⤞⤜ 8 ⤞⤜

SCHOOLING

THE TWO OFFICIAL institutions with which we were connected in our stay in California were both educational—the one was the university, through whose generosity I was in the country; and the other was the school which my son, aged seven years, attended. Inevitably, it was in large measure from his attendance at the school, and our association with it as parents, that I drew my idea of an American education. And not only of American education: the American public school system is clearly much more than a system of teaching boys and girls how to read and write and do sums. Indeed, it was from the school that I drew much of my idea of 'America'—of America not necessarily as it is, but America as the Americans like to believe it might be, it could be, it should be.

In any society a school is much more than a place where small children are taught how to read and write and do sums. In any society a school is probably the best small image of what the society hopes it might yet be: and what is true of any society is, one might say, even truer of American society, where the school system has been given the deliberate and explicit task of 'Americanising' the children of heterogeneous origins that come to it. Everyone knows that American children salute the American flag every morning before school starts, and pledge their allegiance to the flag and to 'the Republic for which it stands, one nation, indivisible, under God, with liberty and justice for all.' Everyone knows this, and everyone finds it a little amusing that the Americans should find this sort of incantation on the part of seven-year-olds necessary and desirable. But when one considers the facts of American size, newness, dispersion and populousness, then the desirability and the necessity for such an exercise by seven-year-olds becomes a little less amusing and a little more self-evident. The explicit Americanness of the Americans is a subject to which I must return, it seems so essential to any kind of understanding of the country.

But there is another sense in which the schools are agents of Americanization—and in which the agent acts with less consciousness than it does when it marshalls the little children in rows and puts them in front of an American flag. And because it acts less consciously here, it acts in a way more revealingly. After all, we knew more or less what the oath of allegiance was about even before we had come to California, but we had to learn what St Valentine's Day (as it was conducted at our local school) was about.

I mention St Valentine's Day because it was a day to which I had never before given any thought at all. In California, however, and with a child at school, St Valentine's Day became of some importance. Even if we hadn't had a child we couldn't have remained entirely unaffected by the displays of Valentine cards at every drugstore and every supermarket; but it was the schools that brought home to us the importance of the Day, and its message. And the message as it was interpreted by the school, was suitably enough, a message of love. Not just a message of love in the way of hearts intertwined and Cupid loosing little arrows at boy and girl beneath the moon, as it was on the cards. No, the message of love sent out by our local school was more general, abstract and significant: it was a distinctly American message of love.

Some weeks before Valentine's Day we received a circular letter from the headmaster of the school telling us that the Day was approaching, and that the school would be happy to help in the distribution of Valentine's cards; but, the letter added forthrightly, no cards would be distributed in class from any particular child to any particular child, unless each child who brought cards brought them for *every member* of the class. Thus, no child would receive more cards than any other: there would be no discrimination in favour of the most popular child or against the least popular child: each child would receive exactly as many messages of love as every other. And to help ensure this happy, abstract democracy of love, a list was appended to the circular giving us the names of all the children in the class to which our son belonged. It should be added that there was also a footnote telling us that the school had no objection to parents or children posting cards direct to other children, or giving cards after school hours—but, so far as the school was concerned with the arrangements, and so far as the school was responsible for them, any favouritism was forbidden.

And the point about this school was that to the best of its power it tried to turn every day into St Valentine's Day. Favouritism or discrimination were all forbidden within its precincts: the school went as far as it possibly could in the direction of goodwill to all, avoidance of direct personal competition between the schoolchildren, or even the comparison of the abilities of one child against another. Conventional report-cards were not issued, I remember, lest the issuing of report-cards should lead to the comparison of the record of one child against that of another. (Instead of a report-card there were individual parent-teacher 'conferences' at which the child's progress or lack of progress was discussed in private.) At the beginning of the year the headmaster made a speech whose substance was that the function of the school was not to pit the children against one another in any kind of race, but to ensure rather that each child did as well as could be expected from him in the light of his own particular abilities. (Or disabilities, the headmaster might have added; but he did not.) 'We want to make your children happy,' the headmaster told the assembled parents; and it was taken for granted that happiness should be a matter of co-operation, collective enterprises, and democratic indiscriminate goodwill.

And I must say that as parents the experiment seemed to us unmistakably successful. The children were happy—our child was, at least—much happier than he had been at school in England. It should be added too that during the time he spent at school in California his writing positively deteriorated, his spelling certainly did not improve, and what progress he made in arithmetic could only be described—at best—as slow. But even if he did not learn much about reading, writing, and arithmetic, he did learn a great deal about the craft of pottery, the distribution of milk from a local wholesale dairy, the rules of fire-prevention, and things like that. It should also be said that he was more at ease and socially adept with adults and with other children than he had been before going to school in California and the difference did not seem to be due only to the passage of time.

The question arises of to what extent the school with which we were associated was 'typical' of schools in California; and it is one which I cannot really answer. I can only say that from what we gathered from others we spoke to on the subject, the Palo Alto School District was generally conceded to be 'good'. But this does not seem to me to affect the general line of argument I am following—which is ultimately about something as large and vague as the American idea of how a society can best be brought together in peace. We never heard a word suggesting that the 'goodness' of the school district was in itself something that was open to question: if it was particularly good, it was good in a way that any American might hope all the schools in the country might one day be. The idea of 'goodness' remained the same, and it is about that idea I am writing: and about the idea as it had been made into bricks and mortar and sheets upon sheets of clear glass to let in the sunlight on the gay, lightly-furnished classrooms; the idea interpreted and nourished by the devotion of the headmaster and staff of the school. And if hard work is any sign of devotion, these particular teachers were indeed devoted.

Theirs seemed to be a vision only of peace, co-operation and goodwill—all of it erected upon a basis of great and continuing prosperity. Because if we were struck by the gentleness and the leniency of the school staff, their unending anxiety that the children in their care should be and should remain together happily, we were struck at least as much by the facilities available to the school to be gentle, lenient, and anxious with. The school was like a treasure-house, a place where the children dipped their hands into wonderful possessions, which were replaced as fast as they were taken out. There was nothing that the school or the children in it might possibly have needed that the children had to do without; and there were, in addition, a hundred other things that the children did not need —that no child could possibly *need*—but were available for them, nevertheless. Probably all schools nowadays give children clay to play with; but at the school in Palo Alto the products of the play were glazed, put in a kiln and fired, so that the children brought home not clay models but pieces of elaborate (and contemporary) pottery work. That there should be radios, television sets and movies at the school was taken for granted.

It was taken for granted that every other few weeks there should be a party at school (to celebrate such events as the opening of a new assembly hall, the visit of an obscure state senator, or merely the departure of any one child from the school to some other); and that from these parties the children should come home laden with a booty of balloons, sweets, papier-mâché firemen's helmets, flags and miniature baseball bats. Then there were the innumerable 'study-trips', when a fleet of yellow buses would carry the children in great noisy loads to visit local curiosities. The children were taught subtraction by the remarkable method of presenting them with ten sweets, and telling them to eat two, and then to count how many sweets were left; they were taught to recognize the letter 'M' by associating it with the marshmallows they were given to eat when the lesson demanded it, and the letter 'P' was the occasion for the distribution of popcorn. Every public holiday was, of course, celebrated by the construction of the most elaborate and expensive home-decorations, every child taking home his decorations, and none of the materials ever being put back into the common pool to be used again. And paper! Every other day the children used to stagger home under great wads of paper covered with their scribblings, or rather just scribbled upon once and then discarded. A single word upon a foolscap sheet was enough for that foolscap sheet to be 'used'; if a single piece of coloured paper was stuck upon a piece of cardboard two feet square the cardboard was sent home for the proud parents to examine. And the paper and cardboard were all of the very best quality, incidentally, stuff with a high, fine gloss on it—none of that soggy, greyish stuff in mean little notebooks which I can remember using as a child, and which I had always thought of as good enough for a child. But in regard to the provision of facilities generally some kind of a climax was reached for me when our child—aged seven, I repeat—came home and told me casually that a whole lot of typewriters had been brought into the 'Multi-Purpose Room' at the school, and that he was going to have his first typing lesson the very next day.

When one is in a position to take for granted such ample supplies of the very highest quality of materials and facilities, it begins to appear almost reasonable to hope that life and human affairs—or rather, and more optimistic yet—that school-life and children's affairs, can be a matter of goodwill, peace and co-operation.

But children being what they are, it is not really surprising that American children seemed to be the noisiest, most demanding in the world, from what we saw of them. Every child was like a little prince or princess of the suburbs, laden with toys, kissed and patted and fondled continually, hardly ever contradicted, rarely ordered about, and never smacked—not publicly at any rate. I was continually being amazed by what American parents would put up with from their children: the children would interrupt any conversation at any time, eat food at all hours, go to bed when they liked, abuse their parents, smash their toys, scream at the tops of their voices at each other, and show no fear of strange adults. Once when I ordered a small boy off my lawn, which he was occupying without so much as a by-my-leave, he took his departure very slowly and sullenly, and at the gate turned and told me that I was a skunk, and then made off with great dignity and at no higher speed. I did not dare to pursue him and hit him across the back of the head, because there were too many mothers on their lawns near by. They would probably have thought the child's remark sweet: I have seen American parents smile at worse remarks made to them by their own offspring. So instead of ordering, American parents plead: instead of threatening, they bribe; and instead of hitting, they turn on themselves and worry, worry, worry about what they have done wrong, that they should want to hit the child in the first place. And all this takes place, it should be remembered, in those 'family-plan' homes where there is no privacy for anybody, where there are hardly any walls or doors to break up the stampede of the children as they run, or diminish the sound of their voices as they scream. And when things get quite out of hand several mothers will get together and load up all their children into several station-wagons and drag the children to the nearest playground, where the children at least have more space in which to do what they did at home.

The world is there to treat the children kindly. School and family are alike in the obeisance they make before the children, in the gentleness with which they handle their charges, in the lavishness with which they provide them with all the things that the great American technology can think a child might need. It is an extraordinary way of dealing with a child who is supposed to grow up into a harried, harassed, grabbing, bolting, hunted, rat-like creature who will eventually die the hideous Death of a Salesman in some heartlessly bright corner of one of the forty-eight states.

That is the American who arouses the contempt and scorn of half of educated Europe: this creature who is fierce, predatory, driven wild by the advertisements in his search for goods, yet who for all his fierceness lives in constant hopeless terror of the Joneses and the due-date of the next instalment of the television set: that is the American, we are asked to believe, that the schools and the methods of child-raising in the homes actually produce. Of course they do not; but this is a secret many Americans seem anxious to keep.

When I think of the people in our suburban street, and the way these people lived together, I can only repeat my conviction that the school offered the best small image of this society's hopes for itself—and of some of its achievements too. It was an image that aroused many misgivings; but I must admit that for me it allayed many more.

About the second educational institution with which we were associated in our stay in America I have to say that when I had seen the roads and the hoardings and the shops and the newspapers and heard the radio and looked at the cars and been called upon by twenty different canvassers, at first I was moved by a sense of mystery that the university should be there at all, and that within it there should be a library, and within the library there should be books, and that these books —good books, serious books, quiet books—should be read at all. Later, when I was to realize that noise and movement and dispersion did not make up the totality of American life, I found the matter less mysterious; but if I am honest I must confess that at first I wondered at the very existence of the place. I asked myself what they wanted a university *for*, how they had found room for it, what they hoped to learn from it. How could they bother with the poems of Wyatt and the history of the French Revolution and the music of Bach and the language of the Italians—here, slap-bang on the El Camino? For the areas of the university devoted to scientific research I could—at a pinch—see some kind of justification, though I had no hope that much disinterestedness and patience could be found so close to the El Camino. But the lecture-halls, the libraries, the music-rooms, the bookshops—I was amazed that they had been erected at all, or that having been erected they had not fallen down out of sheer discouragement and embarrassment at themselves for trying to be what they were, instead of motels, liquor stores, neon hoardings, gas-stations, ten-ton trucks, TV aerials, and several six-lane highways.

And among the discouraging circumstances at first seemed to be the appearance of the students themselves. 'What do the students look like?' my wife asked me, after I had come back from the university on my first day there; and I answered, with no intention of being insulting, but because it was the first, most accurate thing that came into my head—'Like dogs.' The kind of dogs I meant were the short-haired kinds, like fox-terriers and Dobermann Pinschers: all the male students were shorn, unbeautiful, bristling, an endless procession of boys with convict-crops. And their general dogginess of appearance was made more pronounced by the fact that they seemed to wear no clothing at all: the male part of the Stanford student body seemed to consist of three or four thousand young men in khaki or light-blue cotton trousers and shirts. Sometimes one saw a pair of jeans instead of khaki, but that was about the widest variation that could be hoped for: there was never a jacket to be seen, never a tie, never any hair on anyone's head. And all these young men and most of the girls drove around in new and enormous Chryslers, Chevrolets, Fords: there were seven thousand students registered at the university and well over five thousand registered student cars. The Stanford student body was supposed to be particularly wealthy; but it showed only in their cars, not in their clothes, and hardly at all in their manner, which was not really that of gilded youth at all—more that of merely blank youth. Perhaps they were suffering most acutely the pressure of growing-up; perhaps it was at the university that I was able to see one particular group of Americans achieving rather bewilderedly, and without quite

knowing what was happening to them, the quietness of adult-
hood.

Sometimes they made a noise. At a football game in the
Stanford Bowl (seating ninety thousand spectators) the students
all wore special clothes and carried special coloured cardboard
discs which they held up and reversed, and so spelled out giant
letters across the width and the height of the grand stand, and
they yelled together in chorus; while far below them four
cheerleaders, four bandleaders, six Red Indians, innumerable
drum-majors, drum-majorettes and dancing girls, and the
entire one hundred and twenty members of the Stanford
University Marching Band marched, danced, led cheers, led
bands, threw batons in the air, and waved their tomahawks.
And Stanford's opponents on the other side had their own
discs, yells, and assorted marching, dancing, cheerleading,
band-conducting, baton-throwing figures below. There was too
more than a sufficiency of players on both sides of the sideline, all of whom were dressed up in their bizarre uniforms, and
who limbered up like gladiators while their colleagues played.
The spare players on the sideline did somersaults and threw
each other on the ground, and when their turn came they
trotted on to the ground to relieve the last batch. Meanwhile
the gangs of leaders pranced, leaped into the air and cried out
aloud, and the crowds obediently spelled out their letters and
shouted in unison, none of their activity seeming to have
anything to do with the muddled, bitty, mechanical course of
the game as it was played on the green turf in the middle of all
this. Players and spectators made a queer sight in the hot
autumn Californian sunshine; everyone tried very hard, but
there wasn't much joy to it, only a kind of dwarfed, worked-at,
spasmodic vigour, in a too-big, brand-new Roman arena.

Still, it wasn't the kind of noise which could bring the
buildings down. The books within the university buildings were
read, annotated, and discussed; music was listened to; essays
were written; young men and women tried to straighten their
curled American tongues in the effort to produce French vowel
sounds; and an elderly scientist was awarded the Nobel Prize
for the work he had been doing in one of the laboratories on the
campus. At what level the work, discussion, and essay-writing
was being done generally, I cannot really say: I should imagine

F

that most of it was at the level that it usually is in every educational institution of repute, and that a little of it was at the
high level the rest couldn't be expected to attain—patience and
disinterestedness being as rare as they are anywhere, among
any group of people, in any institution.

But my acquaintance with the habits and ways of the university's students was not extensive. The terms of the Fellowship I
had been awarded were very generous, and my time was entirely my own but for one or two two-hourly periods per week,
during which I took part in the Creative Writing classes
organized for graduate and senior undergraduate students of
the English Department. When people in England hear that I
have attended Creative Writing classes at an American university, their faces sometimes positively light up with hope.
Here, one can almost see them thinking, they have something
American which it is altogether safe to patronize, scorn, or
simply laugh at. And there is something so wistful about this
English hope that I am almost sorry to have to say that I am not
at all certain that it is justified.

'Creative Writing' classes are not, of course, by any means
confined to Stanford; as far as I could gather it was a course
that under this name or some other was available to English
students at most of the universities in the country. Whatever
may be the system at other universities, at Stanford the teaching
of it was perfectly straightforward. The class met twice a week in
an elegant room in the library building (the room had been
furnished, and its bookshelves filled, with money from the same
grant that had enabled the Fellowships to be awarded); there
were between a dozen and eighteen members in the class,
including the professor who conducted it. We sat around a
table, while a short story or an extract from a novel in progress
by a member of the class was read to us. Sometimes it was
possible for us to guess who had written the particular piece
before the class, at other times it was impossible; but in any
case we were expected to say whether we thought the piece
good or bad, and why we thought as we did. The discussions
could become quite warm, with people saying harsh things
about the work before them and others—or the author—
defending it. Or the class purred in a unanimity of praise; or

the discussion became a general one about books, writing, favourite authors, almost anything. And the duty of the professor was that of a chairman of the discussion, moderator, leader, summer-up—a duty that frequently demanded the exercise of much tact and care. And that was all. We would drink coffee out of paper cups, and then go home.

Frequently, the stories were predictable and rather dull. Girls without boyfriends wrote stories about girls without boyfriends; boys wrote stories of an altogether excessive masculinity; both girls and boys wrote stories about incomprehending parents. What we did with these stories was the sort of practical criticism that is no longer considered absurd or unlikely by anyone in England; all that was strange about this American variety, of course, was that the practical criticism was exercised upon work that is not in the books—in fact, upon work that usually had very little chance indeed of ever seeing the inside of a book. Often one couldn't help feeling how much better the student's time would have been spent in discussing the work of established writers, rather than their own; at other times, however, the discussions were pointed, relevant, and of use. It depended a great deal on the manuscript before the class. And it must be mentioned that Creative Writing was only one course among many that an English student could elect, and that in all the others the established writers were studied, in the ordinary way.

Yet when the class adjourned the professor's task was not over—he still had to grade and mark the stories and novels handed in to him. And I suppose it is some of the implications of that task of the professor that make the classes seem so offensive and absurd to many people outside America. There are, for example, those who find the idea of 'creative' work being graded or marked in any way an affront to their notions of 'creation' or 'the artistic life'—an objection which I think would have more force if the stories I heard in class had not been as modest in intention and achievement as they were. (What would happen if a genius would enter one of these classes I can't imagine; but I suspect it would be the class more than the genius who would suffer.) A more serious objection comes from those who feel that while undergraduates do make a habit of writing, for them to be able to use these writings as a part of their progress towards their degrees is not merely unscholarly but positively anti-scholarly, defeating the very purpose of the university, which is to train and teach its students, not to indulge them. If students want to write, the argument runs, let them; if they want to criticize each other's writings, let them do that too: if anything is true of undergraduates it is that they will do both these things anyway. But for grown-up men to encourage them to write, and to let their writing be part of the work for which they are awarded their degrees—this is sheer indulgence by all who are involved in it, another example of that peculiarly American want of proportion when it comes to dealing with the arts or the education of their young, the American lack of respect for privacy, loneliness, and single-handed effort.

I agree that it is a peculiarly American lesson that is taught by the existence of Creative Writing classes in the universities of the country; but I would not see the lesson in quite those terms. The lesson is not only that Americans in general are given to spoiling their children; or uncertain about the purpose of the arts and the best way to encourage them; or so democratic by precept and practice that they believe that anyone (who knows?) can be a writer, or is at least entitled to think himself one; or that they are indefatigably optimistic about the possibilities that life offers to any human being. All these things may be true in their way; and the last comes the closest to the point I want to make: but to talk about American 'optimism' as if it were something that here—or anywhere else—hung in the air by itself, is to do an injustice both to Americans and their optimism. If the Americans were merely 'optimistic', then they would be merely foolish, which they aren't; and the existence of Creative Writing classes would indeed only be a matter for English sniggers, which it isn't either.

The point is that there is a level where American optimism is quite indistinguishable from American determination; and that is something at which I find it quite impossible to snigger. To be optimistic (even about an objective as remote as producing or training writers at the universities) is not merely a matter of wanting enough to do a thing, or even of finding enough others who want to do the same thing: American optimism at any level is not divorced in the American mind from the notion of work, hard work. Americans may be wrong in believing that there is nothing they cannot do if only they put their minds to it; but it is very much more than the existence of Creative Writing classes that are dependent upon that belief. Here—as everywhere else in the United States—we meet the American will, strained to purposes as large as the country itself, and as multitudinous as the people who live in it.

⤜⤜ 9 ⤛⤛

QUIET STREETS . . .

TO ONE WHO drives down a highway in California for the first time it might seem that there are no neighbourhoods here, there are no communities, there is no possibility of the development of a sense of mere distinctive localness, let alone the associated virtues of neighbourliness, parochial interest, and local pride. Yet never have I been in a country where so high a value was put on sheer friendliness—so high, and so often spoken-about a value. In exactly the same measure that conditions would seem to make it impossible, the Californians *are* (or consciously believe, and tell themselves, they should be) good neighbours, *are* community-minded, *do* busy themselves with good works locally, *do* hail by their first names their neighbours of a few weeks' standing, *are* untiringly friendly to one another. And presumably should these neighbours be transplanted to other communities, within a few weeks they will once again be hailing their new neighbours by their first names, busying themselves with local good works and local school committees and all the rest. There is something disturbing in the thought; and it is not only that we suspect that a friendliness that lends itself so readily to transportation must necessarily be shallow. It is rather that we are forced to recognize that here we are confronted with something determined and deliberate, a conscious exercise and exploitation of the social will.

And when I turn on myself and ask : is what I have written really true, true of particular individuals I met, I have to answer that there was unmistakably a steadiness, and a determined quality of goodwill about the friendliness we encountered, which cannot be explained or described in any other terms. To talk about it in this way, however, is to make it sound much less attractive than it was. It was exceedingly attractive at its best, and we had a great deal to be thankful for in finding it.

'They're all just the friendliest people in the friendliest country in the world, and they drive me goddam mad,' an

American said to me once about his fellow-countrymen; but it
is worth noting that he and his wife were at the time putting up
at considerable inconvenience to themselves an entire family
of people (my own) whom they had not known really well
before but were nevertheless anxious to help. The difficulty of
illustration I have here, indeed, is one of selection only, there
were so many examples of a warm friendliness, a readiness to
put oneself out for strangers, that we encountered during our
visit to America. There was a lady at the university who in her
free time had started a collection of children's cots, playpens,
pushchairs, which she lent to married students who were in
need of any of these things. There was a lady we met in passing
at a party who happened to hear that we were in need of a
high chair for our younger child; she rang our doorbell a few
days later, carrying a high chair that she had borrowed from
someone else. When an article of mine appeared in a magazine,
a gentleman in Los Altos phoned up and offered to take me on a
visit to a factory, which was relevant to the matter of the
article. The owners of the house we rented could not have been
kinder to us: they went to the greatest trouble to make sure
that we were comfortable, and by the time they had finished
our 'partly-furnished' house was completely furnished. My
wife was frequently asked to coffee by the mothers of children
who were at school with our elder child; and this friendliness
did not fail to find its expression on the official institutional level
too, as far as both the school and the university were concerned.

Honesty compels me to add that though we were very soon
on first-name terms with our neighbours on our left-hand, we
never exchanged a single word with those on the right. Our
neighbours on the left were indeed 'good neighbours': they
were helpful, friendly, and unobtrusive—and they were all
these things in what I can only think of as the American way,
the best American way. They themselves were first and second
generation Americans; the grandfather of the house came
from the South of France, and he told me that he had quite
suddenly decided to come to America, and had left his village
within a week of making his decision, fifty years before. He had
been back to France only once, just after the Second World
War, to see how his family was; and had found everything, he
told me, just the same. 'There is no building there,' he said.

'Not like here in California, where there are new things all the time.' But he said it without pride, even without particular pleasure. By trade he was a carpenter, and when he had first come to California in a boat direct from Marseilles he had worked in the gold mines. Though his eyesight now was poor and his figure was bent, he retained enough of his skill to repair our front gate after my wife had reversed the car into it. He was a quiet, gentle man; his whole family was quiet and gentle; and so too seemed to be most of the other families who lived in our street.

Even the street's one obvious and palpable problem-case was quiet. His name was Bernard, and he lived in a more than usually tiny frame house, no more than one room in width and apparently not more than two in depth. Bernard pottered about in front of this house by day, painting the shingles, mowing the little square of lawn, digging over the flower-beds, and frequently visiting the lady next door to him, carrying a plant in his hand, or a newspaper; or once a new cap which he then put on his bald head to show her how he looked in it. The lady next door seemed to like these attentions; and no one ever spoke of Bernard but in terms of affection or a slightly self-gratulatory pity. Bernard's problems were obviously many, and severe: he was of very low intelligence, he suffered from a severe speech-impediment, he walked badly, and he drank a great deal. He was living, I was told, off a pension—who gave him the pension I don't know: some said 'the social security', others 'the army', others simply 'his sister'. His face was smooth, flushed, and hairless; a few blond bristles stood up from his scalp; his belly protruded; and I never saw him wearing a jacket. He had an old car of his own, which he drove with the greatest care; and he talked to anyone who would listen to him; he tried to sell me a pair of old shoes the second day I moved into the house. And when we had the earthquake that was afterwards reported in all the newspapers, Bernard went from house to house inquiring of everyone how he or she was, and whether or not there were any cracks in the plaster of his house, or broken windows. Speech was difficult for Bernard; he did not actually stammer, but simply opened and closed his mouth in silence before the words emerged in a burst; and in this cramped and urgent way he told me, 'They said on the

radio that this earthquake was *six points*. Gee, isn't that a lot!
Six points of earthquake!—they measured it and all, and that's
what they say, it was so strong. I suppose about ten points would
have knocked over all the houses, or something.' And he warned
me to stand in the doorway if it should come again—that's
what they'd said on the radio—and went off to spread this
warning and his own version of a seismographical recording
further up the street.

So the people in our street managed to live peacefully together, as other people seemed to be doing in all the other
brand-new or older streets of our town; and as they for the
most part no doubt did in all the other suburban towns strung
along those terrifying and deceptive highways.

We were paying about the same rent for our house as we had
paid for our place in London; in fact, considering the cost of
living generally in the two countries we were paying less for
our home in California. Yet it was not only infinitely more
comfortable to live in than our English house; it was aesthetic-
ally more pleasing, it was easier to run, and—above all—it was
more modest, it was quieter in its pretensions. Our house in
London was not at all an old house, by London standards; it
had certainly not been built at a time when it was reasonable
to suppose that the people who lived in it would have many
servants. Yet the basic assumption made in building the house
was that its occupants would have servants, or at the very least
would *look* as though they had servants. This pretension was
totally unreasonable, but it was an unreasonableness in which
I could not see anything admirable; it did not grow out of a
genuine indifference to the opinion of others, but out of an
exaggerated respect for it.

Thus, though our house in London was really very small, in
the kitchen there was a wood and glass panel with indicators
that wagged violently whenever a bell in any of the other rooms
was rung. This was to show the servant (who did not exist) that
someone was calling for attention, and in what room (though
the servant, had she existed, would have been able to tell
by the creaking of the near-paper ceilings exactly where the
entire family was disposed at any time). On the installation of
this important device money could be ungrudgingly spent; but

on making the kitchen a habitable place for a human being to
work in, barely a penny. For the kitchen was where the servant
worked, and why should money have been spent on her, even if
she was never anything but a figment of the class-heated
English imagination? Let the kitchen be small, let the kitchen
be dark, let the kitchen be cold, let the kitchen be dirty—let
the kitchen-maid think about the kitchen: we will think about
the best parlour. But about the English habit of insisting,
even in the house like the one we had, upon a living-room *and*
a best parlour (where no one ever goes) I shall say nothing.
It is like protesting against sham Tudor beams (of these we had
a large supply) or plaster grapes entwined over one's mantel-
piece (we had vineyards of them).

So we were grateful to the American democracy of spirit that
didn't believe itself demeaned by thinking about plumbing,
kitchens, heating—all the low physicality of the house—and
wasn't much concerned with making grand the exterior of the
house. There were no Tudor beams on our American house, not
a single little leaded casement window; there was only one small
gable outside: and the walls in every room managed to stand
up perfectly well without elaborate wainscoting, picture rails,
queer wooden shelves jutting in from every window, bulges-in
and bulges-out of an indeterminate architectural provenance,
mantelpieces as described, and be-flowered wallpapers. It was
not just that our house in California was new. As a matter of
fact, as Californian houses went ours was not particularly new
—nor was it the machinery or the gadgeteering which everyone
associates with an American home that made ours such a
pleasant place to live in. The newer houses and the devices
with which they were filled I have already attempted to describe. But whatever might be said about their 'democratic'
aspirations, of these houses it must be said too that much in
their design was the expression of a modesty and sensibleness
which, to judge from the houses alone, are as deep in the
American character as snobbery is in the English.

The modesty, it should be added, seems deeper by far than
any supposed American passion for wallowing in material
comfort, or for ostentation. For wallowing, of any kind, our
house was not well-constructed. For an orderly and quiet
social life it was. One had the feeling that someone, or many

people, had thought, 'Now, how can people, of such-and-such
an income, with no hope of ever being able to employ domestic
servants, with the problems of raising and caring for a family
of two or three children, and who do not want to work to
exhaustion at this alone—how can they best manage to keep
their house clean, comfortable to live in, and pleasant to look
at?' And a house something like our own was the product of
that thought. There was unmistakably thought in the design
and construction of the house; and no one had been shamefaced
in doing the thinking, or had secretly believed that he would be
more nobly employed in thinking about anything else.

This imaginary reflection that I have put into the minds of
the American architects is not perhaps the most noble topic in
the world to which a group of people can address themselves;
but I cannot help thinking it a more decent one than whatever
obscurity had animated the builders who were responsible for
the design and construction of our house in England. And to
say that this American ambition betrays a middle-class notion
of life or society is not to say anything that frightens me particularly. The United States is a middle-class country—as every
visitor to it, from de Tocqueville onwards, has remarked; and
there are worse notions of life and society than those of the
American middle-classes.

But I am afraid that what I have written about the house
will—despite my denials—serve only to intensify in the mind
of the reader the notion of the American as a wallower, a gross
materialist, a bathroom addict, a kind of lolling, Far Western,
suburban pasha. So it is perhaps worth repeating that I have
not been writing here about mixmasters, garbage disposers,
vacuum cleaners, dish-washing machines, spin dryers, and all
the other large enamelled objects which form the idea of the
American home in most minds. I have not written about them
here because we ourselves did not have them. (We did have a
refrigerator and clothes-washing machine, so I am not com-
plaining of rough living either.) But so much nonsense is talked
of American 'materialism' and 'gadgeteering' and 'labour-
saving' and the rest that it is worth digressing for a moment to
point out that if 'materialism' is a bad thing (of which I am
not entirely persuaded anyway), I know of nothing more
unpleasantly 'material' than trying, say, to wash up too many

dirty plates in a too-small sink with water insufficiently heated by a too-small boiler. If we are going to have hierarchies in our minds of 'higher' and 'lower' activities, let us at least make the effort to know what the hierarchy looks like. And if it is the washing-up that is 'low', then surely the American attempt to make it as speedy and efficient as possible should be applauded.

In fact, of course, it is the Americans themselves who are the most devout upholders of a hierarchy of higher and lower activities; and that is precisely why they have bent their immense zeal and energy into liberating themselves from the human battle with stubborn, resisting matter. In an American home far less time is spent in the confrontation of grubby materials than in any other; and in America the mind of the householder *is* set free for the pursuit of 'higher' ends. (Whether the minds thus set free can possibly pursue those higher ends is quite another question. The poor badgered Americans are beginning to find their freedom a bit of a burden by now; but it is precisely their freedom from a 'low materialism' that is responsible for this, not their immersion in it.)

Were there no really poor people in Palo Alto? There were very few. There seemed to be very few anywhere in the Bay Area. I remember one drive that took us to a queer, rather sinister area, near the fringes of the bay, well away from any other towns, where the ploughed fields and orchards had given way to humps and tussocks of reeds and pools of standing water. Across this marsh they had built a road that lay lavish and cared-for on its causeway; and as we drove along it, there rose clear out of the waste the tanks and stacks and towers of some factory. The buildings were very new, clean, smokeless, and stood on ground reclaimed from the marsh and on a level above it, as the road did. But beyond, and lower than the road and the factory, was a settlement of houses. The houses were clapboard affairs on concrete blocks, unpainted and unwashed; none had a garden; each stood directly on the 'streets' which were all so many lengths of churned-up mud. There was nothing to be seen in any direction but reeds and water and the silver fence of the factory. At the end of one street a wooden shack with sacking in the windows and reeds

growing at its door said in huge but horribly faint red letters:
Dancing, Eating, Drinking. There was not a soul to be seen;
and so it was only by the cars standing in the mud in front of the
houses that one knew this nameless place to be inhabited.

This was the worst we saw near by, though there were a few
other places further off that were as bad in a different sun-
blistered way, and which one should mention, when talking of
opulence elsewhere. So too should a conversation I had with
the mother of our regular baby-sitter. The baby-sitter herself
was a fourteen-year-old girl, and several times when she was
unable to come her mother helped us out. Driving the mother
home one night I made some comment on the prosperity of
the country, and was told that for her part my passenger
wished there were less of it. This I had never heard before;
people occasionally apologized for Californian prosperity, or
made jokes about it, but all of them seemed to accept it as
something inevitable, increasing, and really rather jolly. 'It's
the children who are hurt by it,' I was told now. 'They don't
understand why we can't afford to get all the things they see in
friends' houses. There's so much we can't afford, and really
we don't mind, we're grown up and can understand. But the
children feel cheated. Every time they go away to a party I'm
almost sorry to see them go—I know what they'll feel when
they're there, and what they'll say to me when they get home.'
She spoke sincerely and directly; and though her voice was
quite unlike the strident, harried, keeping-up-with-the-Joneses
voice that I'd been warned I'd hear in the suburbs—and though
indeed I never heard the latter voice—it was nevertheless
chastening to listen to her. But those who had warned me
scornfully against the voice of the suburbs might have been
chastened too, had they heard her, for not the least touching
thing about the way she spoke was her apologetic tone, the fear
she felt lest she was being harried or envious or was trying
merely to keep up with the Joneses.

There is nothing that is simple where human beings are
concerned. Everyone in America is against poverty, and in
America they have done more than anywhere else in the world
to abolish it. Yet this has not made anything simpler for the
Americans—neither for the rich nor for the poor ones. In
America a kind of 'poverty' chases the Americans as fast as

they flee from it—even if it chases them in a motor car. Where
is there an end to it, the Americans are asking, not realizing
that an American asking himself where there is an end to it is
indulging in the greatest American luxury of all. Nevertheless,
it is a good question, and they find little comfort or security
in the thought that there may well be no end to it.

But in the meantime the chase goes on, and quite a merry one
it is too, in California, where it has lost so much of its despera-
tion, and has become a kind of carnival, a free-for-all, a way of
spending time, a kind of recreation. I think these terms are
absolutely accurate in describing something of the spirit in
which most goods are offered in California, and the spirit in
which they are bought. And here I am not talking about
carnival goods, luxury goods, sports goods, goods that people
thought up for want of anything better to keep the machines
occupied with. I am talking about bananas and bread and salt
and children's clothing, the things one buys because one has to.
Even the advertisements, by their very noise and colourfulness
and absurdity, can join in the game, can encourage the pur-
chaser to dissociate his buying from the serious, the calculating,
the simply and brutally acquisitive aspects of his life.

And in some small but not altogether hopeless way there is
a part of an answer here to the question of where it will all end.
The pursuit of possessions can become less the desperate helter-
skelter race it was before, and become more and more of a
game, where there are so many possessions available and so
many different kinds of each. And if the acquisitive instinct is a
low one, but an inescapable one, it seems better to be able to
think of playing with it, than to be forced to take it altogether
seriously.

We used to buy our groceries once a week at a supermarket: we
would go from one supermarket to another, depending on the
'specials' that were offered each week, and depending too on
how energetic we were or how curious we felt about those we
hadn't seen yet. It is with a certain sense of shame that I have
to admit that I *liked* shopping in a supermarket—that central
image of the suburban life in California—and even used to go
into the supermarkets when I had nothing much to buy. They

were all so big and brightly lit, and they always had such
elaborate novelties going on, in the way of advertisement
mobiles suspended from the ceilings or trains puffing on rails
round and about the display shelves, or things on pulleys
coming up and down over your head; once in one supermarket
all the assistants wore little straw hats on their heads, and
around each hat was a silver and purple ribbon that said
'I'm your Uncle and I eat Uncle's ice-cream'. Usually there
was some kind of free ticket one could get for a lottery or a raffle
that the supermarket would be conducting; and, like a man in a
good bookshop, one could browse at leisure among the tins and
the frozen foods and the imported delicacies and the innumerable varieties of ice-cream and the household gadgets and the
magazines and the rows upon rows of glistening vegetables.
No one ever came up to ask you to hurry along, or to ask you
what you wanted, and there was space in the corridors for all
the housewives to pass without disturbing you.

The supermarkets in California—Americans from other
parts of the United States told me—were the biggest in the
country; and certainly none that I saw in New York had
anything of the size and variety of the halls I got to know so
well in California. Halls they were, with their acres of parking-
space around them, with their wide rink-like floors of rubberized
material within, their sheets of glass in louvres, their mysterious
doors that opened so promptly with a hiss when you approached
them and closed with another mechanical and intimate hiss as
you left. And inside these halls was America's plenty. Imagine a
counter seven feet high, with a shelf on every twelve inches
going up, and imagine these shelves six yards long, and imagine
all these shelves for all that length and all that height filled with
nothing but different varieties of *dog-foods!* Imagine another
counter, the same height and the same length and with the same
number of shelves but this one for different kinds of spaghettis
—spaghettis only! And then detergents, or cans marching out
of sight like regiments, or breads or biscuits or vegetables. And
all the meat, wrapped, packed in pretty layers, encased in
massive open refrigerators, with only the blood oozing about
dismayingly within the cellophane of each package, to show
you the low animal origin of what you handled. And the frozen
foods in even colder refrigerators, with pictures on the wrappers

—such pies, such fried chicken legs, such TV dinners, the eye of man has never seen before, and could see nowhere else, to tell the truth, but on the wrappers. And who could ever before have seen so many different kinds of paper? There is waxed paper and greased paper, and kitchen-towel paper, and lavatory paper, and nose-blowing paper, and children's diaper paper, and gummed paper, and paper streamers for parties and paper cups for picnics, and paper plates for the TV evenings, and Christmas paper for Christmas time, and paper to write on and paper to draw on, and silver paper to put over the roast in the oven. Spring-scales hang from the ceiling for you to weigh your vegetables on; there's jelly and junket and a thousand grinning faces of the same grinning baby look out at you along a dazzling line of pre-strained babyfoods. There's shaving soap, there's onion-chopping machines; there's polythene bowls of every size and description, there's egg-fruit and little pots of Swedish caviare; and there's 'Bud' or 'Lois' or 'Cecile' (it says so on their overalls) to take the parcels from you and put them in a box and add up all your prices and take your money away from you, and give you Blue-Chip Redemption Stamps or Green Seal Stamps in return, and your lottery ticket, and a friendly, friendly smile. 'And how are you this morning?' Lois once said to me. 'I'm fine,' I replied; and Lois went on with her addition on the machine, and when she'd finished she looked at me with the same bright smile. 'And how are you this morning?' she asked. 'I'm fine,' I replied; but it wasn't quite as true as it had been the first time she smiled at me and asked her question.

. . . AND QUIET AMERICANS

I HAVE DESCRIBED our reaction after a week or two of exposure to American advertising; our reaction to it when we were no longer quite such newcomers was altogether a different and more difficult matter to write about. For the simplest and most obvious fact about the advertisements remains the most important one: they are not true. They are not true about the goods they advertise, certainly; but in a much deeper and more important sense they are not true about the country they claim to speak for. And the extent to which they are not true is astonishing—there is no other word for it.

Even after a week or two the visitor tumbles to the fact that if the advertisements really did speak for and to California, he would be surrounded by nothing but twitching, writhing, disconnected maniacs—which he very plainly isn't. But he still watches for the twitch, the rise, the response he is sure that the voices and the noises and the colours must be getting. After a year, however, he feels merely baffled; he wonders what on earth the advertisements are about, and who the people responsible for them think they are directed at. They aren't about the California the stranger has lived in for a year, and if they are directed at the Californians he is living among, they seem to be missing their target completely. From wondering and fearing the power of the advertisements, later he is inclined—if anything—to underestimate what is powerful and fearful in them, because he sees they have so little effect.

Americans themselves don't believe that the advertisements are ultimately ineffectual: they prefer to see themselves (or rather, every American prefers to see every *other* American) as advertisement-hunted, advertisement-hounded, advertisement-dominated. I didn't, I couldn't see them like this.

I am touching here at a relationship which still puzzles me whenever I think about it, and which was the central problem to me in trying to get any understanding of my 'America'. The relationship is the one between what may be described as

G

Public America and Private America: which in part is the relationship between the face that America wears on the roads and in the air, and the multitude of very different faces that she wears in the multitude of American homes. And this is a problem that arises not only with the advertisements: it comes up in as acute a form when we try to think of the part really played in America by everything that the mass-media do and stand for; or when we see the violence and assertiveness of American building, American road-making, even of American clothing, and at the same time see the general meekness of the manners of individual Americans. There *is* a relationship, and thus—to return to the advertisements—it doesn't do to dismiss them (as indeed, after staying in America, one is tempted to) as of no importance whatsoever, except as something to see and hear, a phenomenon of as much personal relevance as the Niagara Falls or the Salt Lake Desert. This is as little warranted as the belief that the advertisements really do represent America, or even present to America a picture of a possible society which Americans themselves value very highly. The relationship is a much more subtle one than might be expected —indeed, I can't pretend that I understand it; but so far as I do at all, it seems to me to lie very deep in the nature of what one may still call—without irony—the American experiment.

Among everything else that is persistently advertised on the radio are such things as the need for blood-donors, the importance of the local charitable Community Chest, the Red Cross, courtesy and care on the roads, temperance, the performance of certain patriotic duties—like voting at election times, or keeping one's child at school as long as possible. The time and the space for these public-spirited appeals and injunctions are bought often enough by the bodies which hope to benefit from them; but sometimes they are donated by the radio-station or the newspaper that carries them; or the advertiser of peanut butter or potato chips will slip in an appeal for spastic children alongside. Such appeals are as absurd as anything else which is broadcast; but they are absurd for a different reason and in a different way to the exhortations to buy which precede or follow them. The first point is that they are made over the same radio, say, which for the rest in its advertisements claims to speak only to human greed, and human selfishness and human competitiveness. In the second place they seem to be made without selfconsciousness or embarrassment, or any apparent awareness of the dislocation between these appealsand all the others. And it is possible that in the deepest sense the dislocation is perhaps not altogether so great: that both arise out of the same necessities of the society, out of the same persistent ineradicable social habits, out of the first decision that these people made when they decided to try to live together.

The one thing Americans cannot afford—it sometimes seems —is silence.

This point can be made in many ways; but I shall choose only one further illustration. To a stranger flung down in a suburban Californian town, the appearance of the Americans around him might seem altogether random, uprooted, and equal, and the task of trying to discriminate between them a hopeless one. And as they appear to a stranger, so too, the stranger suspects, do they appear to each other. But these same people attempt indefatigably to make the task of discrimination easier by *naming* themselves and *naming* each other as often as they possibly can. Until I came to California I had never before come across such an insistence upon the importance of the names of individuals. Barely a business transaction took place without an interchange of names, let alone a social transaction. There was not a desk that did not have prominently on it some wooden, plastic or metal contraption giving the name of the person who sat at the desk. Names were worn on clothing; names were even set out in black and white on a painted board at the toll-stations on the bridges and highways, where a car draws up, a hand reaches out and gives a quarter to another hand, and the car accelerates out of sight.

It is not only brands of peanut butter or soap to whom identity is in California a matter of necessary and urgent assertion. And this does help to place in some kind of a context —even if it does not diminish—the noises made by the manufacturers of soap and peanut butter.

The other noises made on the mass-media had their context too. As with the advertisements, I had no choice but to reverse my original conclusions, and to come to a belief eventually in the comparative feebleness of the media (comparative to the noise they make, the attention they demand) in moulding the values and lives of most Americans. And the reason for this feebleness I had to see in what I had originally thought of as one of the strengths of the media: the fact that in America *everything else* is American too.

This fact explains the greater immediate efficiency of the media too, it must be admitted. Inevitably they catch something of the accent, the manner, the rhythm of the life around them, and a rather special kind of impetus as well: it is for all these reasons, indeed, that they are better than their sad imitations abroad. Yet it is little enough of everyday American reality that the media manage to reflect, and despite their greater immediate plausibility, their direct influence is ultimately weakened by being surrounded by everything else American.

The Americans seem positively to have contrived the disjuncture between what they are as individuals and the representations of them that the media are supposed to put forward. The most obvious characteristic of the mass-media is their loudness; the most remarkable characteristic of the sort of Americans we saw under different circumstances and in different places was their quietness.

I suppose it is the measure of the way one can be misled by the noises of the media that I should have been positively surprised when I found out, for example, that so many Americans were extremely fond of gardening—that most quiet of pastimes. But then, when a well-known novelist called a book of his *The Quiet American* neither I nor anyone else saw something slightly ridiculous in the title. Now I wonder why he didn't call the book *The Brown-Haired American*, or *The Blue-Eyed American*.

There are millions of quiet Americans. We lived in America for almost a year, and saw the Americans in the streets and the shops and their houses, and were impressed above all with the quietness of their demeanour. The children and the teenagers might have been 'Americans' as the outside world—under the instruction of the American mass-media—believes Americans to be; but in that case the adults were like well-behaved and well brought-up children elsewhere, grave and quiet and busy and individually unassertive. Americans are—if one must make a single generalization about them—a quiet people.

Even in groups the Americans were quiet. I remember how quiet were the holiday-makers at Yosemite. Or I remember a local supermarket announcing the results of a draw for prizes. There must have been a couple of hundred people in front of the supermarket that evening, their great cars behind them, the glittering supermarket in front of them, and the sun's rays falling flat across the vibrating and tumultuous Bayshore Highway on the right. Here, dramatically, the disjuncture between the people and their styles was displayed: not only in the cars and the buildings and the highway on the right, but in the way the supermarket went about the draw. The prizes had been announced, but as the draws were made the prizes were suddenly doubled, trebled: when a man won a refrigerator it was filled with food, a deep-freeze was stuffed with goods to last an average family for months, to the prize of a stove was added a set of glittering pots and pans. It was all inflated, exorbitant, excessive; but the crowd received it with a calm that even after many months in America still surprised me. It was not that they were *blasé*, so equipped with possessions and stuffed with food that the prizes and the unexpected bonuses meant nothing to them—each of them wanted to win, all right. They took it all quietly because they were quiet; they neither cheered, nor whistled, nor groaned, nor sighed with envy: they were merely interested and amused in the pro-ceedings, and smiled at the jokes the master of ceremonies made, and when it was all over they got into their cars and drove home again, some with prizes and most without. And I remem-ber too how the master of ceremonies made as much as he could of the fact that the prizes were won by 'local' families—in front of his brand-new store serving a brand-new set of tract-houses facing on to the Bayshore Highway.

And in the light of what I have said about the American need for statement and assertion, one is forced to believe that the loudness and vulgarity of the mass-media actually make it easier for the mass of Americans to be as quiet as they are. It is *not* just that they are 'drugged' by the media; *nor* merely that in the violence and noise of the media they find some kind of

vicarious outlet for all that they have to bottle up within themselves. Rather, one feels, do the media relieve them of their
responsibility as Americans to be violent and assertive and
noisy. Re-assured that there is a populated and powerful
'America' of violence and assertion, the Americans themselves
are able to go on being as quiet and as moderate as they like.
They do not want the media to describe them accurately, or to
reflect them, still less to control them. The task of the media is
to make those noises and to adopt those postures which in their
lives as individuals they no longer have room for; but which,
as Americans, they still need to see and hear. In that assertiveness there is security for them; just as there is another kind of
security in their individual quietness.

One of the troubles in dealing with the manifestations and
effects of mass-culture—I suspect—is that the intellectuals who
fear and mistrust it are not immune from power-worship; they
see the power of the mass-media around them, and they worship
by despairing, totally. And it is difficult to attempt to modify
the attitudes of negation and despair without beginning to look
patronizing towards mass-culture in the currently modish way,
or like some kind of apologist. We have all met such fashionable
apologists, or have read what they have written; and we don't
like them. We are right to dislike them, because far too often
they are the beneficiaries and instigators of that which they
pretend to discuss so objectively—the best-selling novelists who
air their views on the least-selling novelists, the television execu-
tives who tell us how much television has done to keep the
family together, the editors of glossy magazines who take the
gloss of their own magazines for sophistication. Or they are the
highbrows without courage, who are anxious to assert their
'humanity' and their 'democracy' by pretending to like what
they don't like, or the highbrows who simply don't know what
they like.

It is not this sort of apologist or patron that I wish to be; it is
no sort of apologist at all. So I will say only that while the
manifestations of mass culture in music, books, magazines,
radio, television, films were generally bad, their effects were
much more mysterious and unpredictable than I would have
been prepared to allow when I first arrived in California. And

at the end of my stay I could not help drawing some kind of hope from the fact that the Americans *did* seem to have a particular and unexpected use for, and a positive way with, the picture of 'America' presented to them by the media.

This is not to say that there are not many people in the United States who spend their lives in pursuit of values as debased and trivial and ugly as those the mass-media have presented to them. The dangerous effects of the assault of the media have been stressed so often that there is really no point in repeating them here; despite all that must be said in qualification, the dangers are real, they do exist.

And no one outside the United States knows of the particular use that Americans seem able to make of the 'America' of the media. Outside the United States, it is the 'America' of the media that is believed to be the true single face of the country. And what a danger this is in itself, when we think of the position of the United States in the world today.

In any case, if it is technology, if it is mass-production and the assembly-line that have made Elvis Presley and his predecessors and successors the figures that they are, it is also technology and mass-production and the assembly-line that are providing some kind of antidote to Elvis Presley and his kind. For the provision of alternatives need not necessarily lie in such desperate and unattractive a hope as that of bringing *The Hudson Review*, say, into as many homes as now take *Life* Magazine. On a Sunday morning in Palo Alto there were really surprisingly few grown-up men sitting in front of their television sets. They were all too busy, doing other things that their wealth (their middle-class, ordinary American wealth) had made possible for them to do. Among these things were gardening, or taking motor boats away on trailers and sailing them somewhere on the bay, working in their garages on their cars, or doing-it-themselves around the house with a hundred devices for a hundred purposes. And the children, for their part, were often enough watching their fathers. Sunday morning in Palo Alto was a very busy day indeed, what with one thing and another, for in addition to tinkering and odd-jobbing, there was a great deal of church-going, family visiting, and just driving about that had to be fitted in as well.

Much of the tinkering and odd-jobbing, it must be said, was of a remarkably high order. The concrete drive-in to an enormous garage might be covered with minute parts excavated from some degutted motor boat, motor car, or electric lawn mower; it isn't an easy task to put up a picket fence, or to lay one's own crazy pavement or even to repaint one's kitchen. And it certainly isn't an easy task to keep a garden as spruce and colourful as most of the suburban gardens were maintained in Palo Alto. Even with the help of a power-driven lawn mower and a pair of shears that click like the door of an expensive car, grass and plants and leaves remain refractory, sluttish, and indifferent; they run to seed, they droop, block gutters, choke each other, lose their colours and die. But those in Palo Alto did not have their own way of things; there were too many grown-ups looking after them, in the sunshine, away from their television sets.

But to have been able to do these things, the grown-ups needed houses of their own, cars of their own, gardens of their own, power-driven lawn mowers, motor boats, second cars to strip to pieces, old refrigerators, and a plentiful supply of paint, screws, nails, wood, tools, and leisure. All these—at least—the culture that had brought them Elvis Presley was able to supply.

One does not want to make too much of this busy and happy-at-home suburban scene; I am sure it will appal some people for whom I have respect; and appal others (whom it is more difficult to respect) who wish to hear only about the television-sodden masses. But one does not want to make too much of it because one cannot help wondering about the depth of the scene, the inward truth of it? How true was it of the inner lives of the people I saw going about their odd-jobs in their shirt-sleeves—that, thus, in their shirtsleeves they had found some kind of privacy, and peace, and fulfilment?

It is a question that only they can answer, each of them by himself, and to himself. The visitor can only say that there seemed to be more peace and privacy in Palo Alto than he had thought to find; very much more than he could hope to find in most other countries in the world.

THE 'BEATS' AND OTHERS

THE SUGGESTION that it might be possible for a middle-class American to find some kind of peace and privacy and fulfilment in a suburban Californian town has been answered by the loudly-expressed views of a group of Californian writers who have recently won for themselves a great deal of attention both in the United States and in Great Britain. I am referring of course to the writers—still centred in California—who were at first known as the 'San Francisco Rebels', but who now go by the name of the 'Beat Generation'.

The Beat Generation came at a good time. Reading the literary journals just a couple of years ago one sometimes got the feeling that all the trend-spotters, the *Zeitgeist* reporters, the people who watch the clouds of dust made by the movements as they wheel, were getting thoroughly discouraged by the alternate silences and incoherencies of the scene they were watching. Nothing seemed to be happening, there were no movements, no trends, no generations, there was really no business offering on the literary stockmarkets. Today, however, the literary brokers and jobbers are somewhat more cheerful. In England there are the 'Angry Young Men'; in America there is the 'Beat Generation'; and both groups not only stimulate chatter at cocktail parties, but also present an occasion for all kinds of predications about 'our culture' in the pages of a great many supposedly serious journals.

The Angry Young Men of England have no relevance to the subject of the present book; but the Beat Generation has. What the San Francisco rebels are in rebellion against is, presumably, the quality of the life I have tried to describe something of in these pages. And because they are, as a group, noisy, articulate, and colourful, it has come to be believed that they are significant —if not significant as literature, at least significant as sociology.

'... After the Second World War there was a convergence of interest—the Business Community, military imperialism, political reaction, the hysterical tear- and mud-drenched guilt of the ex-Stalinist . . . American intellectuals . . . This ministry of all the talents formed a dense crust of custom over American cultural life—more of an ice-pack. Ultimately the living water underneath got so damn hot the ice-pack has begun to melt, rot, break up and drift away to Arctic oblivion. That is all there is to it.' This quotation—describing the genesis of the Beat Generation—comes from an article by Mr Kenneth Rexroth, introducing an anthology, called *San Francisco Scene*, of the writing of the 'rebels'. On testing it, however, Mr Rexroth's 'living water' turns out to be so tepid it couldn't melt a pound of butter, let alone an ice-pack. It would be merely embarrassing to quote from most of the poets of the rebellion, their poetry being for the most part so remarkably innocent of rhythm, of a true feeling for the weight and value of words, or of sustained thought, that one can only wonder at the prestige of verse, that it should continue to attract so many people who have no particular talent for writing it.

But there is always Mr Allen Ginsberg to throw into the breach; and in fact one cannot accuse Mr Ginsberg of being incapable in quite the same way as most of the other poets who contribute alongside him to the rebellion. His poem 'Howl'—reprinted in part in the anthology, and the longest single poem in Mr Ginsberg's own collection, *Howl and Other Poems*—is perhaps the most notorious of the documents produced by the Beat Generation. (*Howl and Other Poems* has not yet been published in England—possibly because of censorship difficulties.) Mr Ginsberg's poem tries to be what its title proclaims: a howl of rage and defiance, in long Whitmanesque lines describing people who, for example,

'. . . *were expelled from the academies for crazy & publishing obscene odes on the windows of the skull,*
    who cowered in unshaven rooms in underwear, burning their money in wastebaskets and listening to the Terror through the wall,
    who got busted in their public beards returning through Laredo with a belt of marijuana for New York,
    who ate fire in paint hotels or drank turpentine in Paradise Alley, death, or purgatoried their torsos night after night . . .'

and so on, and so on, relative clause piled upon relative clause for page upon page. Now it is clearly insufficient to say in condemnation that this writing is incoherent, frenzied, frantic, self-indulgent. It is all these things, but the people who admire it are likely to turn around and say, 'Well, that's what it's *meant* to be.' Mr Rexroth, in his introduction to the anthology has already described such remarks as 'favourable' to the poem. Apparently for many readers it is Mr Ginsberg's very frenzy and incoherence that are to be admired. They see his poem as a defiant assertion of the individual spirit—an assertion against what Mr Ginsberg in the same poem calls the 'Moloch' of 'Robot apartments! invisible suburbs! . . . blind capitals! demonic industries! . . . monstrous bombs! . . . Pavements, trees, radios, tons!'

'"Howl",' Mr Rexroth assures us, 'is the confession of faith of the generation which is going to be running the world in 1965 or 1975.' I think that in making this comment Mr Rexroth is true to the spirit of the poem. And it is precisely for this reason that I must say, so far from finding 'Howl' defiant and anarchic, and all the rest of the things of which Mr Rexroth (and Mr Ginsberg, if one can judge from the internal evidence of the poem) would be so proud, 'Howl' strikes me as being pathetically dependent on a concurrent movement of literary opinion, on the *Zeitgeist* as familiar ally, on the anxious support of those who make it their business to jump as the 'generation' jumps. So far from finding the poem individualistic, it seems to me afraid to stand on its own legs. In its very first line 'Howl' simply puts its fingers between its teeth and whistles up its friends.

For who are the people who are doing the terrible things to themselves that Mr Ginsberg describes in all his relative clauses? He tells us, in his first line. 'I saw the best minds of my generation destroyed by madness, starving hysterical naked,' he announces; and it is this hopelessly bald and unsupported assertion that he expects to bear the weight of the rest of his poem. So we know where we are already. It seems that Mr Ginsberg could not write his poem about one suffering soul: it had to be about nothing less inflated (and companionable) than a 'generation'. What kind of individualism is this, exactly? What kind of a rebellion is it? Couldn't 'Howl' have howled about one mind, one man?

The answer of course is no. For if 'Howl' had been about

one mind, one man, it would have been a far more difficult poem to write. Restraint and thought would have been forced upon it; the poem would have demanded a facing up and a dealing with particular experience that Mr Ginsberg—for all the violence of his language—has preferred to shirk. And the paradox is that it is only the truly and unfrightenedly individual in art that can ever give us a general truth of description, a picture of a place, a time, a country.

Howl and Other Poems is dedicated to several people, among them Mr Jack Kerouac, the author of *On the Road*, who is described by Mr Ginsberg as the 'new Buddha of American prose, who spit forth intelligence into eleven books . . . creating a spontaneous bop prosody and an original classic literature . . . All these books are published in heaven.' Now, however, as we all know, *On the Road* has been published on earth as well, and very successfully too. The publishers of the American edition of the book inform us that, 'After World War I a certain group of restless searching Americans came to be known as the "Lost Generation". . . . For a good many of the same reasons after World War II another group, roaming America in a wild, desperate search for identity and purpose became known as the "Beat Generation". Jack Kerouac is the voice of this group, and this is his novel.'

Or—as Mr Kerouac himself puts it, through the mouth of his narrator—'I pictured myself in a Denver bar that night, with all the gang, and in their eyes I would be ragged and strange and like the Prophet who walked across the land to bring the dark Word, and the only Word I had was "Wow!"' When Mr Kerouac says 'Wow!' he can occasionally convey a sense of innocence that is affecting. But he is truthful enough about himself when he describes his insistent intention in the book as that of a prophet, a bringer of some large truth about America and human experience. The hero of *On the Road* is a man called Dean Moriarty, the prototype of the Rebel, San Francisco-style: he is a great lover of women, an ex-juvenile delinquent, a talker, a petty thief, a taker of drugs, and—we are repeatedly told—a saint and an angel. '(Dean's) criminality was not something that sulked and sneered; it was a wild yea-saying overburst of American joy; it was Western, the west wind, an ode from the Plains, something new, long

prophesied, long a-coming (he only stole cars for joy-rides) . . .
A western kinsman of the sun, Dean.'

This is a note that recurs with all too great a frequency
throughout the book, and nowhere does it carry any more
conviction than it does the first time we hear it. Moriarty is
never 'explained' or examined by anything more than this
kind of rhetoric, and so, despite all the strain and emphasis, it
remains purely a private conviction of the author that car-
stealing is a form of yea-saying. The conviction might well be
more persuasive if we were allowed in Mr Kerouac's work—and
that of his friends—to see a little more of the kind of people
from whom cars are stolen. And it would certainly have been
of help if Mr Kerouac's rebel-hero, who talks about life like
this—'We give and take and go in the incredibly complicated
sweetness zigzagging every side'—were not such a bore. (Nor
is the boredom he causes in the least relieved by the author
immediately assuring us, 'There was nothing clear about the
things he said, but what he meant to say was somehow made
pure and clear.')

We have to take it entirely on trust that the conditions of
American life are such that if one wants to say 'Yea' to life
one has to indulge in the violent and delinquent activities
of Mr Kerouac's heroes. It is with this demand upon the
reader that *On the Road* finds common ground with 'Howl', and
with Mr Rexroth's introduction to *San Francisco Scene*; but we
cannot possibly respond to the demand when there are so few
signs that these writers have been serious enough to look
determinedly and honestly at the America around them before
leaping to their alarming conclusions. And this is true too of
the rest of those writers of the Beat Generation whose work I
have read—with all their violent assertion, and emptiness of
response to the external world. There is no sense of a clear
individual gaze at any one aspect of American life in all their
writing: instead, at best, we find some tedious satire of 'American' values: or we find poets who seem to imagine that we will
obediently feel scorn and horror when they name 'suburban
bedrooms block on block'; 'two cars in every garage'; 'supermarket suburbs', and the rest of their empty imprecations.

This kind of thing can hardly be dignified by calling it
a criticism of American life. In fact, it seems to me a great

deal *less* subtle and devious, and a great deal more crudely predictable, than the life it is supposed to be criticizing—the life actually lived within the supermarkets and suburbs. The outsider cannot but be struck again and again by how totally these 'rebels' accept some of the most vulgar of the received ideas of 'America' as the truth about America. 'I'm obsessed by Time Magazine,' cries Mr Ginsberg in one of his poems, and he speaks perhaps more truly than he knows.

I suppose it should not come as a surprise that at a time of great prosperity and great insecurity there should be writers—and readers—who seek to flatter themselves by believing that it is in images of despair, danger and rebellion that they see themselves and their society reflected. This is a tendency which is not by any means confined to San Francisco, or even to the United States. Self-pity and self-admiration of this sort comes all too easily in a time like the present.

But the truth is that we are entitled to despair or howl for rebellion only after much harder work than anyone of the Beat Generation has bothered to do. The success of these writers illuminates nothing but the bankruptcy of our fashionable literary life: certainly it is little enough else that we can learn from them about California, or about America at large.

No, if one does want to find out something about America by reading poems or novels it is much further—and further back—than the Beat Generation that one should go. However, it must be admitted that anyone who comes as a stranger to both England and America cannot but be struck at first by how much less he seems to have learned of contemporary America from the classic American novelists than he has learned about contemporary England from the English authors. Half the fun of living in England, one sometimes feels, is just the delighted confirmation of the expectations one has derived from literature. Dickens and George Eliot and even Jane Austen still seem to have far more to do with the England of today than, say, Hawthorne has with anything in California. Indeed, Hawthorne or Melville or James or Mark Twain has so little to do with anything one can immediately see, that the expectation that any one of them might do so begins to look naïve in the extreme.

California, after all, is almost as far from New England as England itself is; and Melville wrote for the most part about the sea or the Marquesas anyway—these are the things one begins to tell oneself in reproof. And then, formidable and distinguished though the great American novelists are, their writings are not only smaller in bulk than their English counterparts, but are of a significantly different kind—a kind in which the observation of appearances and manners has never counted for as much as it does in the English novel. And it is inevitably the superficies of appearance and manner that a visitor is most likely to notice.

Yet—for all that—there is a continuity of a particular kind that the mountainous facts of geography and history have not broken—and the suspicion that one has learned nothing from the American authors about modern California is unfounded. There is a persistence, though unlike the English persistence it has little physical about it, and is not to be found directly in matters of appearance, ways of speech, or overt social relationships. This continuity or persistence, it seems to me, may most simply be described for the moment as the extreme self-consciousness of Americans about being Americans.

It is obviously not a simple matter, no matter how simply a year's residence may tempt one to describe it. And an outsider is probably more aware of this self-consciousness than he should be, and tempted to read more into it than he should, for people always explain themselves to an outsider much more than they do among themselves. Yet the English, one might say exaggeratedly, have the air of always being faintly surprised and amused that there are any people in the world who are not English; the Americans on the other hand, seem always a little surprised that they are Americans. Or if not surprised, at least aware that there is something so special in being Americans as to demand exhortations and explanations, reproofs and warnings, to each other on the subject. In fact, there seems to be a positive campaign about America that actively and continuously engages the institutions of government, the schools, assorted public bodies, and all the media of communication; this is the simplest and most vulgar expression of what operates as busily on many other levels of sophistication.

The self-consciousness that in the books of Henry James and

others takes the form of a debate between a postulated 'America' and a postulated 'Europe' is hardly the same thing as that which at election-time sends out the Boy Scouts with placards shaped like the Liberty Bell, urging the people to vote because it is the American thing to do; but there is a connection between the two, and it is not a tenuous connection either. And in however crude or reductive a fashion it must be done in this context, we cannot avoid assimilating both kinds of self-consciousness to what we have sensed of the American will. On their level the Boy Scouts illustrate it; on quite another, the great novelists anatomize it, each in his own way. Melville may have written about a whale-hunt; but Ahab's boat '*rushing ahead from all havens astern*' is—as D. H. Lawrence described it—'the ship of the white American soul.'

THE PYRAMID AND THE SUBURB

AT FIRST I used to wonder how typical were my experiences in California of life in the United States at large; but later the whole question seemed to grow less and less relevant to the kind of idea of America that I felt forced upon me, during my stay in that one part of it. Living in California I came to feel that any one state would have been as 'typical' as any other, because all the states were different and because they were all alike, and because they all could have contributed with equal legitimacy to whatever idea I might have had of the country as a whole. Perhaps this is merely another way of saying that though in California I felt myself to be living in a 'province' of some kind, the longer I lived there the more convinced I became that I would have felt the same thing wherever I might have lived.

New York clearly seemed to be the city that published the books and made up the advertisements and generally set the intellectual fashions. But to a newcomer in distant California, trying to bring into some kind of order his idea of 'America', this did not in itself manage to make New York a more import-ant, more central place, than Kansas City or Omaha, where New York's fashions were accepted or opposed or distorted or ignored—each of these reactions being a fact not only in the history of one particular fashion, nor only in New York's relation to Kansas City and that of Kansas City to New York, but in the relation of each of them to what one had to think of as 'America'. Of course Washington—to take another example—was the place where the laws were made and interpreted; but even that did not seem to make Washington a more central place than Council Bluffs, Iowa—and not only because Council Bluffs helped to send to Washington the people who would make the laws, but because Washington was hardly a city at all, being an abstraction, belonging to no state, voteless, set apart from every other city in the country. Yet at the same time it seemed absolutely necessary to reverse the argument too, and

H

add that precisely in its very singularity Washington was 'American' too, and typical and essential in its Americanness. Of course Los Angeles was the place where they made the movies, but that did not seem to make the city itself any kind of a 'centre'—intellectual, moral, or artistic—to the millions of people across America who watched the movies. Detroit was a place where they made motor cars and Chicago and St Louis were places where they packed meat, but neither of these were ever thought of as centres of any kind either.

This inability to find a centre, an obvious, potent capital city of any kind, where the main stream of American life gathers itself in special fullness, variety and power, is related closely enough to the sense that the newcomer has of America as a sheer sprawl, a kind of hopelessly disordered and populous backyard to an ideal, imagined world of societies, nations, and communities. If there is one figure, one image, that is central and ineradicable in our thinking it is that of society as a single great pyramid of power and prestige. Kings, courts, aristocracies, capital cities, classes in sharp definition against one another, may have ceased to exist in Europe in an effective sense; but something of the old authority, the old styles, lingers on as more than a ghost, remains a kind of hope in the relation of group to group and class to class in each surviving European nation-state. The divisions and the ultimate unity of society continue to be seen in terms of intimate, interresponsible duties and privileges that are older than the conservative or revolutionary hopes of re-making them.

But the United States—it need hardly be said—has never had a king, never had a court, never had an aristocracy, never had a capital city, never had classes in sharp and prolonged definition against one another; and their absence can be felt outside the history books. In the United States the figure of the central pyramid of society has neither past nor present relevance: the country cannot be seen—or even attempt to see itself—laid brick by brick into a single form, with a single base, a single summit. It has always been, one can say, too big, too new, too prosperous, too egalitarian in spirit and achievement, with too many people of diverging origins and interests spread over too many thousands of miles.

And what history and geography enjoined upon the United

States has been sedulously maintained and encouraged—even
by forces that one would have imagined to have the opposite
effect. To come to Palo Alto, California, is to be overwhelmed
by the feeling that one is clinging to a fragment of settlement
floating in a great sea of other and equal fragments; and this
feeling of sundering and equivalence is made stronger by the
passionate localism of the press, by the repetitiveness of what
one is likely to see on the roads, by the amiability and the
indifference of the strangers one meets, so much like the amiability and indifference of one's own neighbours, and by the
availability everywhere of the goods one wants. The availability
and the uniformity of the goods and services provided by the
greatest industrial machine the world has ever known makes *not*
for a sense of cohesion—as might be imagined—or not only
for that at any rate, but also for fragmentation and dispersion,
for sprawl upon sprawl.

This seems paradoxical, on the surface, when we consider
that industry demands before all else rapid and efficient
communications that must bring everyone within reach of
everyone else, no matter how big the country may be. But
why—to put it in its very simplest terms—should I have gone
to San Francisco when there was nothing that I could not buy
in Palo Alto, as a result of those same rapid and efficient communications? And this is just one example of the way in which
industry and prosperity serve the sense of dispersion, remoteness
and disinterest in what is elsewhere. We have to revise some of
our notions about the centralizing and cohesive effects—even
mechanically—of industrialization. We have already seen that
the suburban style of life, with its ever wider dispersion of
people and their interests and investments, owes itself directly
to that prime effect of the country's industrialization: the
availability of the motor car to practically everyone who wants
one, and the availability too of the roads to carry all those cars.
And I would suggest (inevitably perhaps, in the light of my
experiences—though without trying to introduce in this way
a claim for their typicality) that the figure to be used in describing the direction in which American 'society' is developing
is that of the suburb, not that of the pyramid. It is the flat
dispersion, equality, and separation of the suburb that most
approximates to my idea of the shape of American society; and

for this we have, in part at least, America's industry to thank, or to blame.

Once again one is impelled to say that such a situation is new, so new that the Americans themselves don't seem to know what to make of it, how best order can be made out of it. Americans read European books, and most of their ideas of the forms a society can take are European. They seek a capital city, they seek a centre in which all the social pyramids can converge, and in which they can all ascend. And the most important fact about American 'society', or whatever name we wish to give it, is that it has not and never can have the kind of centre for which they seek. So the Americans declare that there is no American society, overlooking the very one that sprawls at their very feet. It is a new kind of society—it is a society that has none of the obviously, the 'naturally' cohesive characteristics that we have known all other societies by; but it is one nevertheless. If only—one wants to say, in the lecturing tone that visitors so easily assume in America—the Americans themselves would realize the uselessness of their search for what their society can never have; if only more of them would *look* hard at what was around them, and would try to find the lines of force of the society that is there; if only they would realize the intense differentness of what they are about, then the talk about newness and differentness would not be left so much in the hands of the leader-writers and the propagandists, whom one disbelieves anyway.

It is just possible that the kind of 'society' which is emerging in America can never—by its very nature—know itself in the way that other societies have known themselves; and thus never have within itself the possibilities of order, dignity and nobility that come with such self-knowledge, and that we perceive so readily in every civilization but our own. It is possible, I say; but I don't know. I hope not anyway, because if it is true the outlook for none of us is a cheerful one. And when anything is as new as this dispersed, egalitarian and prosperous American society, it seems a bit premature to me to give it no hope at all of self-discovery and self-knowledge, of order, of dignity.

There is a curious irony in the fact that as Europe grows to know less and less of what is happening in America (and the

Americans themselves are in large measure to blame for this),
so the Americans in their search for identity and self-knowledge
seem to turn more and more to Europe. And of course, looking
at things through European spectacles they fail to find in
America what they are looking for; and give their voice to
confirm the European suspicion that there is nothing in
America, and that America is socially a desert, a neon-lit
vacuum and all the rest of the stuff that any second-rate
European intellectual will parrot out with a knowing look in his
eye and a patronising tilt of his head. The temptation one
has is to cry out to the Americans, 'If it's a society you're
looking for, for heaven's sake forget about Europe!' but that is a
mistake. The American couldn't forget about Europe even if he
wanted to, and it would be a disaster if he did. So all one can
say is, 'Don't look for Europe in America, because you won't
find it. Look for something else, it is there, though no one
knows what to call it.'

But the American can turn around indignantly and say,
'What do you want of us? That's what we're trying to do all the
time. Look at Hawthorne, look at Henry James and Henry
Adams, look at Mark Twain, look at—look at—look at *me*,
standing here and listening to you.' And the American is quite
right. His attempt to give himself a name—and his readiness to
listen to the names that other people give him—is precisely
one of those things that justify the assertion that there *is* something that can be called a society in America, even if it is a
society different in kind to any that the world has known before.

Things in other countries might seem 'just to happen'; but in
America I continually felt that things had happened because
people had had ideas about America as it was and as it should
be, and ideas too about themselves as Americans. It is curious
that this country, where the relation of abstract ideas to facts is
such an urgent one, should be the same country that looks to the
newcomer like nothing so much as a mindless sprawl. Or
perhaps it is not curious after all, because there are a great
many Americans, each with his or her own idea of America.

A GREAT GOOD PLACE

IT MUST BE remembered that America is a country that was thought about before it was inhabited. The descendants of the Puritan settlers (to use the most obvious case) may make up a very small percentage of the population of the United States; but the Puritan settlers were immigrants of a very different order to the people who were sent out to South Africa in the days of the Dutch East India Company, or the convicts who were sent to Botany Bay in Australia. The convicts had no choice; and the South African settlers came with no intention other than that of planting vegetables for the ships of the Far Eastern spice trade. But the Puritan settlers came with *ideas* of what America should be, and the intention of realizing their ideas.

I was surprised when I read in the history books that the United States was the oldest republic in the world; and also the country with the oldest written constitution in the world: we think so much of America as a 'young' country—as indeed it is, in comparison with the countries of Europe. But in formulating and making explicit ideas about itself, America is old, older even than its own settlement.

This is not something accidental or merely interesting. It is relevant both to the generalized idea any visitor will form of 'America', and to every aspect of American life which he is likely to see or in which he will participate. Explicitness in formulating ideas and intentions is a habit which can be traced back carelessly to the country's very first settlers making up an idea of America before they had even seen the continent; it is a habit that in the United States seems to persist in fields far (and yet near) from the abstract, the moral, the ideological. It persists—to choose here comparatively minor matters—in American social manners: which are not in the least crude or simple as people sometimes say they are, but explicit, rather; it persists even in the patience with which the Americans put up with the nonsense of the advertisers. The atmosphere of the country is one that encourages statement, statement, statement,

of any kind. Sometimes it even seemed to me that the way
Americans speak—so fully and doggedly pronouncing out
every syllable of the English words they use—is yet another
example of their enduring need for explicitness, for full statement. This peculiarity of enunciation is presumably derived in
part from the fact that English was for so many Americans an
acquired tongue—and that fact, in turn, has a great and obvious
relevance here.

What, indeed, is there that Americans are not forced to be
explicit about, in their relationships with one another and to
their country? What—I asked earlier—do such things as
neighbourhood, community, or society mean here, in America?
And the answer seems to be statement, and statement again.
There was nothing but a few Red Indians in America when
people started thinking about it, and making statements about
it; and once they came to America there was nothing there—in
the way of human society—but what they thought up and
spoke up for themselves. And to reinforce this necessity for
formulation and statement, making it keep its prime importance
in American life, has been added every one of the major factors
in American history: from the expansion westwards to the
mass migration in the early years of this century, and the
enormous success of American technology. For every new event
threatened a return to the original disorganization and nullity
of the country: every new event needed thinking about and the
statement of the problem once again, as the very first settlers had
had to think about what they would do in a country of their
own when once they got a country of their own. The conditions
of the country encouraged nothing but chaos, disorder, and
disruption; but the history of the country had given the people
who lived in it a weapon to use against chaos, disorder and
disruption; and they have used it, and it seemed to me, used it
with remarkable success.

The weapon was statement; what they made explicit they
made orderly—or rather, what was made explicit was made
possible, and from the sheer fact of possibility, order could come.
The possibilities were new ones: they derived from different
conditions to any which the world had known before, and when
they were acted upon their embodiment was different. And the
difference is to be found precisely in the explicitness which was

not merely the ground of action, but in the very style of action, the movement of the people towards one another.

There was no possibility of the development in a country as big as a continent of the kind of local patriotism that could flourish in the small countries, counties, cantonments of Europe. But there could be stated the idea of the United States of America; and once the idea was formulated it became possible for the country to come into existence as something for which patriotism could be felt. There was no possibility that immigrants could feel a mutual loyalty to one another in the instinctive and unspoken way loyalties between people had been preserved in Europe. But once the immigrants could have a common loyalty to the idea of their country, as it had been made real through being spoken about, made real in being spoken about—then the immigrants could become loyal to one another as Americans. And what was true of the nation or the country as a whole was true too of the sense of community, of society, even of mere neighbourhood. And it remains true in its way under today's conditions in the State of California, where I lived, among all the cars and the brand-new houses and the endlessly repetitive gas-stations and radio-stations and main streets and super-highways.

Americans themselves often believe that America as it is today is a country that has no past, that America discards its past immediately it is done with it; but to me it seemed unmistakable that there is a continuity, a habit of mind and will which is specifically, particularly American. And this continuity has arisen precisely from the very lack of a continuity of an instinctive, unspoken kind. There is nothing that Americans take for granted about their country and themselves; they are always starting afresh. They have never ceased to have to say the words—the same words, under different circumstances, meaning different things. And just as they are continually, determinedly *becoming* Americans, every time they open their mouths to say the word, so too they are continually, determinedly *becoming* neighbours, communities, every time they move, every time they say the words of friendliness to their new neighbours. And this is true too of each community as a whole. It is precisely in the tension of becoming and never arriving that the people know their identity as Americans: because their history never ceases, and there is always something new to become, a new demand that circumstances exact and that they are determined to do their human best to meet.

When we think of loyalty, pride, patriotism, neighbourliness, even the language, we like to think of them as instinctive, simply there because they have always been there, carried by each generation to the next without thought. And what is instinctive, immediate, having no need for conscious thought or self-consciousness, we believe to be deeper and truer than what has to be expressed in words and thought about and discussed. Probably we are right in this belief. Inevitably, in a country like the United States there is a loss of that instinctive sense of order and place and manner that can control the actions, the words, the very movements of the hand of a simple Zulu from the kraal, or a well-bred English girl.

But there is a gain as well. The gain—it seems to me—is that through explicit statement and self-consciousness the Americans have made a particular contribution to solving or at least dealing with a problem that vexes more countries than the United States. Dispersion, anonymity, rootlessness are not problems that are confined to the United States alone: there are big new cities and big old cities everywhere, and people live in them and work in them and have their problems of identity and loyalty. But just as these problems—on the face of it—are so much more acute in America than elsewhere, so too the Americans have gone furthest in their attempt to give substance and coherence and reason for their millions living together. That has always been their attempt, and in confronting the new pressures of modern industry and communications the Americans paradoxically have an advantage, in having been threatened with incoherence and dismay so often before.

The Pilgrim Fathers did not come to America because they were anxious to establish a one-man, one-vote democracy on the best modern pattern. But though the ideas of the Puritans of New England are not ideas which might find favour with most modern Americans, they *were* explicitly and by intention ideas about what the Puritans believed would be a Good Society, a holy society under God. They came to America because they thought of it as a possible Promised Land. And the idea of America as the Promised Land, as the great good place, has persisted too; inseparable from the very notion of 'America' through every change of belief as to what is social or spiritual 'goodness'. The one idea cannot be considered apart from the other; they were born together and they are still locked together in the American consciousness, at the profoundest level. And let us not forget that in America the profoundest level is likely to be the explicit level, so bound up and simultaneous are all these factors that we are trying to consider in apartness.

By intention, at any rate, America remains Utopian; the Land is still the Promised one, to everyone who has managed to come to it. Inevitably this imposes a strain on people's awareness of themselves and their society. America is not a Utopia, and never can be one; and much of the bitterness which Americans feel about America, much of the disillusion and despair and self-destructive moral doubt in American writing can be traced to this sense of failure that a Utopian expectation must bring in its train. (And it is surely not an accident that to express their doubt many of the great American writers should have used allegory, parable, and fable, the least explicit of literary forms.) It is an impossible thing that Americans are asking of themselves and their country; and they know it; and they continue to ask it.

The Rule of the Saints was an attempt at a Utopia quite different from that which might be imagined today by the inhabitants of a suburban town like Palo Alto, California. The American hope for a Utopia today is in general, I suppose, a 'liberal' one. We use the word 'liberal' so loosely; everyone has his own catalogue of attitudes which he would describe as liberal. But common to them all I think is the sense of hope for the future, a belief in the possibility of human betterment, and the desire for this betterment to be shared by as many people as possible, and not to be confined to any group or class within a nation, or to any one nation over all the others. And the nature of the betterment is both material and spiritual; indeed the distinction between the two is blurred, for though the latter is considered the more important, it is seen as being inevitably dependent on the former.

This is a crude enough summary of what can be labelled the 'liberal' idea or attitude; but it is through the holding of the idea in some such crude form that most Americans can be called liberals. (And often enough they hold the *idea* even though they themselves may be emotionally of a thoroughly conservative, backward-looking temperament.) I was continually being surprised at the extent to which a liberalism of this kind seems to have penetrated every area of American life. The United States is a country where liberalism—so far from being embattled and defensive—can be described as the official ideology of the country, the one to which everyone in some measure believes he subscribes, or should subscribe. And this is true in spite of the position of the Negroes, in spite of McCarthyism, in spite of the banning of this or the other book or teacher. Indeed, one of the reasons why the anti-liberal forces in the country often find their expression in spite and malice and unpredictable outbursts of violence is because theirs are the embattled attitudes, disapproved of socially and looked down upon intellectually.

People outside America—liberals particularly—are remarkably ignorant of the extent to which the ideas and attitudes of liberalism have become the accepted ideas and attitudes in the United States. This ignorance is partly due to the conviction of intellectual American liberals that they have failed in their task, when they see how much prejudice, bigotry and violence there is in American life; and this conviction of failure is in some respects an honourable one, being an expression of the high hopes of American liberals, of their high sense of duty. But there is another aspect of it that is less attractive; among liberals, as in any other group, righteousness and self-pity are well-served by a sense of official powerlessness, or permanent unavailing opposition.

The liberal mind is one that is particularly at its ease with the habit of taking thought before action, of finding out what it wants to do by stating what it wants to do; just as it is most ill-at-ease with what is instinctive, intuitive and irreducible in the actions of men. To an outsider it seems no wonder that liberalism of the kind discussed here has had the success it has in the United States, the promised, and talked about land.

. . . . .

So even here, in this liberalism, in this cast of the American character at apparently its gentlest, we are aware once again of a deployment of the conscious social will, with all the tenacity and effectiveness given to it by American history and the conditions of American life.

And we see it too when we return to the disjuncture that I have commented on before. I would, I suppose, describe my generalized idea of the American as someone who is friendly, quiet, helpful, anxious to like and be liked by his neighbours, bland, saltless, and amiable. But no one has ever accumulated the immense material possessions of the Americans out of sheer goodwill, nor have the tall buildings, the bridges, the great highways, the cars—all the vast established machinery of America—been created on that inspiration alone. In order to be well-liked no one advertises his product among the hundreds and thousands of others to the point where if any serious attention were paid to the advertisements the country would be inhabited entirely by incoherent, twitching maniacs. When one sees the advertisements, the goods, the cataracts of cars pouring out of a big American city at four and six and eight abreast at sixty miles an hour, the roads and the bridges leaping over them to other great black roads—when one sees these things one is prepared to imagine any deliberate strength to a people who build and manage to live among these things.

Bland? Good-humoured? Neighbourly? Co-operative? Amiable? How can they be, one asks; and replies at first that perhaps the Americans one meets can afford to be these things because others have made it possible for them. Perhaps the Americans were *once* what the newcomer—seeing what they have accomplished in the manufacture and disposition of goods —imagines they must have been. Could it possibly be that the present generation, enjoying the fruits of the labours of others, can afford to take things easily, and to take each other more easily? Perhaps the American character has changed; no longer masterful and rapacious, it can be bland and co-operative on what the mastery and rapacity of the past generations have handed down to it.

And probably there is some truth in this; but one would be happier about it as a resolution of the mystery were it not that the Americans *still* seem to work as hard as they ever did, as they ever could have, as anyone could. Whatever else the Americans might be doing, they are still widening their roads, putting more cars on them, throwing bridges across bays and rivers and roads, building houses and filling them with a fantastic range of devices, building taller and yet taller skyscrapers, and more aeroplanes and television sets; they are still selling things to one another as hard as they ever could have. The material achievement for which the advertisements can stand as a symbol is continually and determinedly maintained, re-distributed, and surpassed.

And all by a people who manage at the same time to appear modest, friendly, full of goodwill, and jaded with possessions. There is such a curious lack of connection between what these people do with material things and what they themselves seem to be; the relation between American habits, manners, and socially accepted ideas on the one side, and the continuing American achievements on the other is one that escapes an outsider. It is as if these builders, drivers, manufacturers, workers, salesmen do not know what they are doing when they work, how unlike their own idea of themselves is what they accomplish. To the outsider there seems at first to be a kind of blank spot in the American soul, something unrealized and not even striving for realization, but content merely to lie low, keeping the peace in each heart between the builder of bridges and the casual good neighbour.

But later one comes to believe that the good neighbour and the builder of bridges are both servants of this single, indomitable American will—which, in this world, wants the best of all possible worlds, which wants and believes it can get not less than everything.

No wonder there is an air of violence in America. For all the gentleness with which it so often finds expression, the American will is implacable, and can never rest.

⤛ 14 ⤜

CONCLUDING

WE HEAR so much talk about the 'Americanization' of the world that after having been to America I think it worth recording that I no longer know what the word is supposed to mean. How does one 'Americanize' the English—if anything of what I have said about America is true? And the French? And the Germans? And the Russians? And the Boers? And the Indians, Arabs, Israelis, and Japanese? Elvis Presley can bawl his head off from every loudspeaker in Tokyo, and Tokyo won't thereby be Americanized; and Johnnie Ray can twitch on every cinema screen in Bangkok and the Siamese won't thereby be Americanized, and bearded Zulus in the streets of Johannesburg can drink Coca-Cola until their bellies are distended, and they won't thereby be Americanized. Something will be happening to them all—is clearly happening to them all, English, French, Zulus, and the rest—but it isn't 'Americanization'. To Americanize any group of people is clearly a much tougher proposition than people generally care to admit; I don't see how it can be done unless this group of people inhabits a country much like America physically, and go through the same historical experience as the Americans, with the same recurring psychological and moral patterns. Unless, in fact, they go to America, they aren't going to be Americanized; and I suggest that whatever is happening to them be given a different name, in the interests both of clarity and amity.

For it would help both the Americans and everyone else if both sides were to realize how unrepeatable the American experience is, how unlikely it is that the Americans can export their experience on their continent as easily as they export their Coca-Cola. The United States has arisen out of special historical circumstances which have shaped and reshaped the manners and habits and the ways of thinking and social relationships of the people living in it. It is these manners and ways of thinking among the people that are alive and elusive and disconcerting and hopeful among the brutally tangible mass of material things,

the all-too audible shrieks of the media—and are what no one
thinks of when they talk of 'Americanization'.

Of course those who are most ready to pull the longest faces at
'Americanization' are precisely those who prefer to believe that
Americans have no social relations, no ways of thinking, and no
manners. But these grimaces merely show up—they do not hide
—the nullity behind the distorted features. Far too often the cry
of 'Americanization' is an attempt to burke a local problem by
giving it a dirty foreign name, a way of despairing without
injuring the self-esteem of those who raise the cry.

There are problems that every society has in common with
every other: problems of culture, problems of social relationships, problems of community and identity. But the contour of
each problem is different to the country that has it: no more
than the Americans are able to, can the people of any other
country escape from their own history. Certainly we are all in
for a highly industrialized society of one kind or another;
certainly there is going to be change upon change coming upon
us all. But 'Americanization'? Almost, I wish it were true, and
not a bogey-story.

Because if there is going to be change upon change coming
upon us, then we *can* learn from the Americans. If we want to
make the future share in what is valuable from the past, we
must learn to use our full minds upon the forms we wish our
society to take; above all, from the Americans we can learn a
new respect for our own wills, whose exercise need not always
result in enmity, destruction, and despair. For none of us now is
there any way of survival, but through will and awareness.